5 WEEKS TO SELF-CONFIDENCE

5 WEEKS TO SELF-CONFIDENCE

A GUIDE TO CONFRONTING YOUR INNER CRITIC & CONTROLLING YOUR RELATIONSHIP WITH YOUR THOUGHTS

LYNN MATTI
MA, LPCC

ROCKRIDGE
PRESS

Interior and Cover Designer: Erik Jacobsen
Art Producer: Sara Feinstein
Editor: Daniel Grogan
Production Editors: Andrew Yackira and Erum Khan
Production Manager: Holly Haydash
Author photo courtesy of © Leticia Andrade.
All illustrations used under license from iStock.com.

ISBN: Print 978-1-64152-662-3 | eBook 978-1-64152-663-0
R0

To the children who continue to suffer from blaming themselves for things that are not their responsibility and are beyond their control, and to the adults who believe themselves unable or unworthy of the life long-dreamt and wished for. May this book help in some small way.

CONTENTS

INTRODUCTION

For many years, I suffered in silence. I turned first to controlling and perfectionist behaviors and then to alcohol. No matter my internal discontent, outwardly I was fine—I was okay—because drinking, controlling people and things, and then later taking anxiety and sleep medication were not only permitted but seemed to be wildly encouraged. They were acceptable, albeit not always effective, ways of coping with my daily stressors. Life flowed on and on. Until one day I realized something that frightened, confused, and intrigued me. Numbing myself with alcohol and medication, and trying to control everything and everyone was not simply a release or a bad habit for me. After years of practicing these unhealthy patterns, they had become *the only* way I coped with life, stress, and all my inner insecurities. Drinking, medicating, and trying to be perfect became my confidence, my self-esteem, my identity.

My internal world became overpopulated with questions about who I was, what I wanted, and how I got here. Who was I without my wine, Xanax, and "getting it done right" persona? At my core, I felt disconnected from the most important person in my life: me. Why? I started to dig deep for the answer through therapy, and what I found shocked me. I unearthed a long-held belief that I was unlikable, most likely unlovable. After all those years of performing for others, I didn't understand, accept, or truly love myself.

A thought kept pushing toward the surface: I wanted something different. I needed something different! We are so used to solving our own problems with our own way of thinking, believing each of our thoughts to be true, that we don't realize this tends to perpetuate the feelings and life we find ourselves wanting to escape from. We confuse being needed and successful—the stuff of self-confidence—with authentic self-esteem. But they are *not* the same thing. Confidence is measured by our behaviors and abilities, supported by the feedback of others. Self-esteem is felt and experienced from within. Esteem is the alignment of our beliefs, values, and self-concept. It is our relationship with our self.

For most of my life, I was confused by my need for both attention and solitude. I often felt overwhelmed in the very leadership roles that seemed to come naturally to me. It was common for me to seek out people, events, and activities that seemed to drain me of all energy. I was filled with toxic self-doubt, rarely sleeping well due to all my worry and rumination. This self-doubt was torturous to endure and eventually felt like it *required* numbing.

During my 20s and 30s, I worked with psychotherapists, untrained helpers, and mentors to guide and assist me. Unfortunately, most seemed to embrace and want to fan the flames of my strong confidence in the areas of organizing, planning, sales, and leadership, while minimizing or even discounting my growing anxiety and depression. My focus became building my self-confidence using all the regular external markers of achievement and success: appearance, income, and possessions. These shiny conquests and achievements continued to temporarily soothe my internal angst and eclipse my deeply buried personal core values.

A reckoning came in my 40s. A hard truth needed to be faced—I'd missed the window of opportunity for having a child. My world had become one of self-doubt, alcohol, anxiety medication, and lack of sleep which inevitably led to the four in the morning questions: Who am I? Why am I like this? What should I do? Where am I going in life? What is my purpose?

After 46 years of frenetic activity, I decided to get some answers. First, I needed to get free from the substances that had stolen my mind and rewired my brain. It took two years of therapy and group counseling, plus hours of curiosity-driven education and learning. I practiced the art of letting myself feel all the human feelings and ground myself in the world I lived in. Next came the true transformative work of learning who I was from the inside out.

During my early sobriety, I quickly realized that much of what made alcohol and other substances attractive to me was their numbing effect. I had been afraid to be alone with my thoughts, which mostly revolved around the fear of what others thought of me and my actions. I had no peace or contentment, which is exactly what I craved! An overwhelmingly terrifying thought began popping up in my mind, over and over: Go back to school to become a psychotherapist. Ugh, talk about lack of confidence! Thank goodness for the strong support network that comes with getting clear of alcohol and drugs.

Beginning graduate school at 46 is no joke. It's pretty challenging to sit in a classroom for the first time in 25 years. Despite this, I became a psychotherapist, and I was naturally drawn to those with anxiety, substance use disorders, and self-esteem issues. A truly satisfying part of my life has become helping people learn to believe in themselves and overcome something that once caused them great anxiety.

Over the past seven years, whether it's been through my therapy and coaching practice, speaking, or my podcast, *SoberSoul Recovery*, I have helped thousands of people learn to be more self-confident and build lasting self-esteem. Each person arrived with different life goals, but each one shared a common desire to move beyond self-doubt, worry, and fear.

I believe our world is experiencing the most consequential epidemic of our lifetime, one of impoverished authentic self-esteem and self-confidence. So many of us are struggling with overwhelming negative thoughts, guiding us toward self-doubt, rumination, and resentment of others and ourselves.

These negative feelings live deep within us, initially planted and nurtured both consciously and unconsciously by our caregivers as warnings intended to protect us and help us cope with conflict and danger. Yet during our earliest and most vulnerable years and moments of emotional development we begin to internalize these warnings, often distorting them and causing them to slowly change into emotional land mines. These are then often triggered by the typical ongoings of life, like relationships, work, our social lives, and day-to-day stressors, building to a crescendo, demanding an immediate and often irrational response. Research strongly links low self-esteem to a variety of mental health and quality of life problems, such as poor or unhealthy relationships, overuse of substances, unhealthy behaviors to cope with life, and depression and anxiety.

This book has one simple goal: to help you develop and build a healthy and growing understanding of and relationship with yourself (self-esteem) in order to let your true nature and strengths shine in the "other world" (self-confidence). I will show you ways to accept, trust, and love yourself, and to believe in your self-worth.

This book is meant to be a guide through the early days of your adventure toward fortifying your self-confidence and into building measurable, lasting, and sustainable self-esteem. Over the next five weeks, we will tackle how to get started on your personalized journey. I'll teach you proven goal-setting techniques backed by science and real-life practice, as well as how to stop your inner critic from distracting and derailing you! You'll learn effective tools for changing your relationship with your thoughts and understanding the beliefs and values that drive your behavior. Finally, you will discover the one area of your life which I've found, through years of practice and many clients, has the most long-lasting effect on your self-confidence and esteem. Learning and practicing these skills will offer you the ability to write that blog post, start that business, have those difficult discussions, and live a more courageous and purposeful life. And don't worry—you won't be alone on this journey. I'll be right there beside you, cheering you on!

CHAPTER 1
Understanding Your Self-Confidence

The loudest voices in our heads often belong to self-doubt. Attending to them is a courageous, purpose-driven, and often formidable pursuit. During the process, you will likely feel disheartened and scared, but what these feelings are telling you is that you are on the right path. Acknowledging these mostly undesirable and often suppressed feelings is part of your journey.

USING THIS BOOK

This book is my collection of the best and most effective techniques for overcoming self-doubt. I've broken them down into five parts which can be accomplished over five weeks. My goal is to provide you with a simple flow of ideas, examples, and exercises that are easy to put into practice. I ask you to be willing to explore what you read here by investing your time, effort, and energy into applying these techniques in the areas of your life that need your attention.

THE SCIENCE-BASED METHODS I USE

We'll be using two well-documented types of behavioral therapy that have been proven effective through numerous studies.

Cognitive Behavioral Therapy (CBT) is a widely used and studied approach that focuses on developing targeted coping strategies for solving your current patterns of problematic thoughts, attitudes, and beliefs. The key to CBT is exploring optimistic and realistic thoughts that can help teach you how to take control over how you interpret and cope with your everyday environment/world.

Acceptance and Commitment Therapy (ACT) is also well researched in reducing the problems associated with "overthinking," such as anxiety, depression, and substance use disorders (SUDs). ACT differs from CBT by noticing, accepting, and embracing emotions just as they are, as it is the denial, numbing, and struggle with emotional pain that causes us to suffer.

BEST USED IN REAL LIFE (IRL)

I will be giving you IRL impacts each week in the form of quizzes and activities with the intent of identifying your habits, personal attributes, and thought patterns. Additionally, helpful exercises will give you insight into how to put all this new knowledge to work in your daily routines. This book is created to be used as a stand-alone teaching tool, but will prove even more effective if you add these three things:

* Immersion – You have to *feel* the change, not only read it. Feelings come from being fully engaged in this experience.
* People – You will experience the most improvement if you use all of the information to practice with real, live humans.
* Action – By practicing what you learn, you can replace feeling stuck with feeling accomplished. Reading books have given me mammoth ideas, strategies, and new ways of thinking. The commitment to practicing what I read was the real game changer for me.

A NOTE ABOUT THERAPY

My clients come to see me for help with a wide variety of mental-wellness issues and concerns, including anxiety, relationship problems, disordered eating, depression; and substance use, overuse, and addiction. It is estimated that only 41 percent of adults with any sort of mental health concern receive some sort of professional care. There are many reasons for this trend, but the main causes are stigma and lack of time and funds.

I wrote this book to offer the same proven methods I use with my private coaching and counseling clients in a concise, straight-forward, and short-term format. To get the full benefits, all I ask is that you open your heart and mind to learning and practicing something new.

CHAPTER 2
Beginning Your Journey to Self-Confidence and Self-Esteem

Now that you understand a bit about what I do and how I aim to help you, I will share the broad strokes of what self-confidence and self-esteem are, and how through mindfulness and practice you can improve your relationship with yourself and others.

CONFIDENCE AND ESTEEM: DEFINITIONS AND DIFFERENCES

When people use the terms "self-confidence" and "self-esteem" interchangeably, it drives me a little crazy. While they are related and have an impact on each other, they are distinctly different human characteristics. You can have high self-confidence and low self-esteem (pretty common) or high self-esteem and low self-confidence (not so common). Let's start with the basic dictionary definitions:

SELF-CONFIDENCE:

* An acknowledgement and appreciation of your abilities
* A belief in your ability to succeed in what you attempt
* A sense of self-trust

SELF-ESTEEM:

* A sense of confidence and satisfaction with yourself
* Respect for yourself as an individual
* A belief that you are worthy

Clearly, self-esteem and self-confidence work as a team to influence how we live our lives and how our worldview is shaped. When they are in balance and finely tuned, they have positive impacts in all areas of our lives: relationships, communication, work, and play.

Our lives are a roller coaster of positive and negative feedback. While we may strive for peace, prosperity, individuality, and equality, the human experience is far from perfect. We all view ourselves differently, and this impacts how we view the world around us. Each of our perspectives, especially about ourselves, drives how we behave in our daily lives. You are the creator of your perspective. Someone can have an impact on that perspective, but they cannot entirely change the way you view yourself. Only you can do that.

A mirror is a great metaphor for both self-confidence and self-esteem, depending on the perspective you take while looking in the mirror. Do you see yourself through the eyes of others or through your own eyes? What do you rely on to feel good about yourself? Do you prioritize how you see yourself or how others see you? This is your source of validation, either external or internal, and it will play a huge part in reading and working with this book.

YOUR RELATIONSHIP WITH YOURSELF

Ask yourself this: What is the common denominator in every interaction you have with the people around you? Yep, it's you. This is why where you get your validation from is so important. Most of us spend a good deal of time worrying about how we speak, listen, respond, act, react, give, or take from others. How much time do you invest in doing the same with yourself? In this book, we're going to focus on you, both in terms of getting the external validation you desire and the internal validation you need.

Without question, the most important relationship we develop in our lives is the one with ourselves. Yet most of us spend the majority of our waking and sleeping moments nurturing other relationships at the expense of our internal relationship with ourself. We live in a time when there is great emphasis on digital citizenship, and social media interaction is, well, addictive. I often find it difficult to remember what it was like before we were so connected to the world yet so disconnected from ourselves. This constant bombardment of images, subliminal ads and messages, and the constant fear that we are missing out on something takes us further and further away from self-acceptance, gratitude, and love.

If you cannot love and give time to yourself, how can you expect others to? You are worth every moment, every positive thought, each minute you give yourself that helps you build and live a happier life.

Now that you have a clearer understanding of what self-confidence and self-esteem are and how they are different, let's determine your personal starting point. Take your time and go easy on the self-judgment! Sure, this is a way of figuring out which areas may need attention, but it's also a way to acknowledge your strengths. Carefully consider each of the following statements in the next activity. Circle 1 if a statement is true for you most of the time, 2 if it is true for you at least some of the time, and 3 if it is not usually true for you.

HOW MUCH DO I BELIEVE IN MYSELF?

I feel like I can handle problems if I work hard enough. **1 2 3**

I believe my goals are realistic and achievable. **1 2 3**

I can manage unexpected events that come up. **1 2 3**

I can find a solution to most problems I have. **1 2 3**

I spend a lot of time trying to handle my fear and doubts. **1 2 3**

I don't often stop short of finishing projects or tasks. **1 2 3**

I am comfortable with and do well under pressure. **1 2 3**

I believe that hard work will eventually pay off. **1 2 3**

Asking for help is easy for me. **1 2 3**

My thoughts do not paralyze me from moving forward. **1 2 3**

My abilities and wisdom grow with effort and experience. **1 2 3**

My actions and behaviors usually line up with my values. **1 2 3**

If someone doesn't like/approve of me, it doesn't bother me. **1 2 3**

Whew! Now let's dig into your score:

Mostly 1s: You are doing a great job learning from your struggles and experiences! This book will help you find ways to build on your strong base of self-confidence and deepen your self-esteem practices for improving your relationship with yourself.

Mostly 2s: You are in a good place for recognizing some quick growth! Though you sometimes recognize your skills and accomplishments, you often focus more on what you "should" be doing better. In this book, you will have access to tips, skills, and practices to identify and build those overlooked areas.

Mostly 3s: You are likely hoping for more, more, more confidence and esteem! This book will help and support you in having more compassion for yourself, and nurture you beyond obstacles and setbacks. Together, we will walk you through how to set and achieve meaningful goals by identifying and using your strengths, skills, and unique talents.

HOW DID YOU FORM YOUR SELF-ESTEEM AND CONFIDENCE?

As you now know, there is a difference between self-confidence and self-esteem. They tend to interact differently at various times in our lives. One way to decipher these two ways of seeing yourself is to think about what motivates you. If you are *externally motivated,* you perform or engage in an activity as a means of earning a reward or avoiding punishment. You don't always do something because you enjoy it or find it satisfying; you do it to get something in return or to sidestep something that is very unpleasant or uncomfortable. When you are *internally motivated,* you do something or behave some way because it's rewarding, and you like the activity or behavior and desire to do it for yourself to make yourself happy.

I love to start a session with a client who is struggling with these concepts with this question: "What did you love to do when you were eight, nine, or ten?" It gets at the heart of what we were able to do without being self-conscious of our actions. This taps into our confidence level and is how we fine-tune our external motivation. I loved to climb trees and would often want to race my brother and other boys to see who would reach the top first. It was so much fun to challenge my friends because I had the confidence that I could either beat them to the top or come very close to matching their pace.

Famed psychotherapist Erick Erickson theorized that we humans progress through a series of stages as we develop and grow. According to Erikson, between the ages of six and 12, you learn how you compare to your peers—how you socially "measure up." In certain situations, you will learn that your abilities are better than those of your friends and that some talents are highly prized by others. Naturally, this leads to feeling confident. Yet some of us discover we are not quite as capable as other kids at schoolwork or socializing, which leads us to feel inadequate.

Your self-confidence and self-esteem are shaped by many circumstances that are out of your control. Our ideas and beliefs about ourselves are created via repeated experiences. These ideas have an enormous impact on how our character traits develop. They determine when we really feel secure, what we think is funny, who we're attracted to, and virtually every other component of our daily experiences. How we store these beliefs is random and often illogical. As a result, we have difficulty examining why we see our lives and surroundings the way we do.

How we paint our reality is heavily influenced by our genes, culture, early childhood experiences, and life circumstances. Our body chemistry, including our "safe place hormone," the neurotransmitter serotonin, can be altered due to genetic or cellular variations. Temperament is also linked directly to our genetic makeup; some of us are naturally more cautious and reserved and others are more outgoing.

A number of individual life occurrences and experiences may also lead to feelings of insecurity and sometimes even unworthiness. Significant trauma such as physical, sexual, or emotional abuse severely inhibits the development of healthy self-esteem and confidence. Difficult and stressful early life experiences such as illness, emotional neglect, frequent or sudden household moves, changes in the family structure, or a death in the family have also been shown to have a negative effect on a child's sense of self-confidence and esteem. How we see ourselves is directly related to how we learn and experience interactions and reactions from our parents and other influential people in our lives.

Below are the most common types of low self-confidence and esteem. You will probably relate to one or more of them in multiple areas of your life, family, work, and social activities.

The Critical Over-Thinker ruminates and runs through do-overs, options, and catastrophic scenarios 24/7.

The Shamer is hard on themselves, but easy on others, and mostly resents it.

The Comparison Maker measures their body, mind, and soulfulness against others, not trusting their own opinions.

The Worrier Warrior is frequently fearful of challenges, which causes them great anxiety and inner turmoil.

What each of these styles has in common is a focus on external forces out of our control. The scale is tipped toward not making mistakes and away from learning from them. Most of us come into the world with pretty high self-esteem and confidence. As our minds and bodies grow and develop, we learn that others may withhold affection and love from us. In turn, this creates a disordered way of thinking about our personal value or our worthiness in the eyes of others. Without emotional guidance from our caregivers, we are left to develop and rely on coping skills such as predicting other people's behaviors (The Critical Over-Thinker), blaming ourselves for other's behaviors (The Shamer), mistrusting ourselves (The Comparison Maker) and isolating with avoidance (The Worrier Warrior). These are the unfortunate consequences of living your life motivated by external forces. Luckily, we humans have an innate ability to adapt and change—if we decide to! Read on, my new friend.

SELF-CONFIDENCE AND SELF-ESTEEM LOOK GOOD ON YOU

One of the most rewarding aspects of my career has been helping people achieve healthier inner lives supporting more purposeful outer lives. So, what are you going to get out of this book if you put the work into it? While I cannot guarantee that all of these incredible things will happen to you all at once or even at all, this is what is possible:

* You will enjoy, like, and value yourself.
* You will be able to make better decisions.
* You will take the time you need and learn to be with yourself.
* You will handle mistakes without blaming yourself or others unfairly.
* You will be able to assert yourself without feeling guilty.
* You will recognize, name, and accept your strengths and weaknesses.
* You will show kindness and compassion toward yourself.
* You will believe you are good enough and that you matter.
* You will discover what you want, need, and desire, and learn to believe that you deserve these things in life.

LACKING SELF-CONFIDENCE AND SELF-ESTEEM TAKES A TOLL

In big or small ways, the impact of low esteem and confidence can dramatically reduce the quality of your personal relationships, resiliency, self-care, work life, and overall physical and mental well-being. But you are here to get yourself the awareness, insight, tools, and support to produce meaningful change in your life.

HOW TO LEARN AND GROW

Let's get a little nerdy together. In the last decade, there's been an explosion of information gleaned from studies of our brains. I call myself a "neuro-nerd," which I loosely define as someone interested in and actively learning about neuroscience breakthroughs. Have you ever found yourself drawn to someone because they seem to speak without second guessing themselves and appear so darn comfortable and trusting of their words and decisions? Scientists are digging deep and studying what our brains look like when we are confident and have good self-esteem. You can literally see your "brain on confidence." More importantly, they have proven that we can train our brains to be more confident!

In this book, we will use ACT and CBT to increase your psychological flexibility. All of your personality traits, including your self-esteem and confidence, live in your brain. A complex web of neurons work around the clock to transmit information from our brains out into the far reaches of our bodies and then back again. Recent research has not only confirmed the overall effectiveness of ACT and CBT, but also shown that self-directed work like reading books and practicing the methods can also be very effective.

WHY FIVE WEEKS?

Many people have outdated ideas of what therapy is, as evidenced by how many of us put off going until we are in emotional dire straits. Access to mental wellness therapy is difficult for many of us, and finding the time, money, and energy can be so overwhelming. That's why, for the last decade or two, professional counselors have been trained in Solution-Focused Brief Therapy (SFBT). I often incorporate this approach with my primary approaches, CBT and ACT, because most of my clients are high-functioning and know they want to see me for five to eight sessions. This is why I have chosen a five-week course of five core concepts toward better self-confidence and a foundation for lasting self-esteem.

It is important to clarify that five weeks is a relatively short period of time. If you actively work and practice what you read in this book, you'll put yourself on the fast track to improving your self-confidence while also forming a core practice of habits that build self-esteem. In order to build sustainable self-esteem, we need to focus on changing the patterns your brain is used to performing by taking different actions and creating different, repeatable results. You can go ahead and read this book all the way through, but I highly recommend taking your time through the whole five weeks, experiencing each chapter as you would five counseling sessions.

WHAT TO EXPECT

Creating sustainable change takes awareness, self-reflection, time, and practice. I have found that there are core concepts which work to increase our overall self-esteem and confidence, and each of them deserves individual attention. Here's how I've broken things down in weekly "sessions":

Week One: Setting Goals. You'll decide on your desired outcomes and learn methods for building a strong foundation of confidence and esteem.

Week Two: Meeting and Confronting Your Inner Critic. You'll raise your awareness of your inner dialogue and learn how to change the tone of your worst critic.

Week Three: Transforming Your Relationship with Your Thoughts. You'll learn to recognize patterns in your thoughts and build an alliance with that voice working to defeat you.

Week Four: Beliefs and Values. You'll unearth and assess the ideas that have put your behavior on autopilot.

Week Five: Communication. You'll exercise the most important muscle in your self-confidence and self-esteem building program.

Included in each weekly session are morning and evening exercises—easy things you can practice as you go about your day, on your commute, while you take your kids to school, or when you wake up or are ready to fall asleep. They're a mixture of fun ways to visualize and be mindful of yourself.

HOW WILL YOU KNOW
YOU'RE GETTING RESULTS?

I have to say, this may be the tricky part. (I often recognize improvement in my clients long before they do!) But it's an important part of growing our esteem and confidence to acknowledge our own strengths. Here are a few ways to measure your progress for yourself:

✳ You begin to act and speak more assertively, expressing your needs with less guilt.
✳ You are more aware of what is happening at the time it is happening.
✳ You start up an old hobby.
✳ You say yes to things you would not have before.
✳ You begin to prioritize your need for sleep, exercise, fun, and food.
✳ You understand and practice self-compassion.
✳ You become more curious and develop a desire to keep learning about yourself.

If you've made it this far, I want to congratulate you! You have begun the process of taking your inner life a little more seriously. This is an important step toward finding out what matters to you and developing the tools to create a stronger bond with the most important person in your life: you. The choice will be forever yours; you can choose to do nothing more or you can step into exploring, curating, and developing to your fullest potential and purpose. Are you ready? Then what are you waiting for? Turn the page!

CHAPTER 3
Week One – Setting Goals

This week, we are going to:

* ✱ Learn why setting goals is good for your self-confidence;

* ✱ Explore your strengths;

* ✱ Dig into your relationship with goal setting and the science behind setting and achieving goals; and

* ✱ Walk you through proven step-by-step goal-setting techniques.

We'll build on:

* ✱ Your current level of confidence and esteem and where you want to grow and go;

* ✱ Your strengths, successes, and achievements; and

* ✱ Your commitment to yourself.

When living in Washington, DC during the 1990s, I met a man who continues to be an inspiration to me. Tony was a vibrant and talented young attorney in the office where I worked, and we became fast friends. He slowly shared his story with me.

He told me that people seemed to assume that he had always been confident and sure of himself. But when he first moved to DC, he had zero confidence. He was hyperaware of his short height, waifish body, and the fact that he was gay and hiding it. He was overwhelmed with negative self-talk, felt weak, and figured nobody would ever want to have a relationship with him. He thought moving would offer him more freedom, but he continued to avoid groups or being in social settings, always worrying about what other people thought of him. Though he knew he was good at his job, he had difficulty speaking up in meetings because he was always thinking and rethinking about how he should say something. Tony became isolated and sad, and he suffered bouts of anxiety and depression.

About two years after his move, he decided enough was enough. He'd reached a crossroad of deciding to stay the same or try something new. First, he made a commitment to himself to ask for help and found a therapist who he liked and got along well with, which began his personal journey of self-improvement. They worked on ways to improve how he accomplished things, starting with small daily tasks, gaining awareness of his internal negative voice. He went on to learn more about his beliefs, attitudes, and values, which gave him insight into how to develop meaningful goals based on what he needed and wanted for his life, plus some specific steps he could take to reach them. His therapist helped him whittle down his goals so they were challenging yet doable.

Tony worked hard to change his internal voice and mind-set, trying out new ways of thinking and speaking to himself. Within a few weeks, he found the confidence to share his true self with some close friends (including me). Over time, he was able to learn tools to better understand himself and how to communicate his needs to others.

WHAT DO YOU WANT TO ACHIEVE AND WHY?

Goal setting is something that we hear about all the time, right? New Year's resolutions, 30-day challenges, self-help gurus, and so on. Most of us are not fans of setting goals because we often feel defeated when we don't attain them. Before we get down to the nitty-gritty of why this is, let's first take time to do something we usually don't take the time to do: explore our strengths.

WHAT ARE YOUR STRENGTHS?

Knowing what your strengths are and using them often will give you a self-confidence boost. Yet because humans are naturally negatively biased, your brain focuses more on what you are not good at. Getting clearer about what our strengths are and how to use them effectively is the purpose of this exercise.

Set aside some time to work with your loved ones and with yourself to figure out your strengths. Grab a notebook or write your answers on your device.

* What do you enjoy doing?
* What do your family and most trusted friends say they enjoy/like about you? You can use what you already know, but you can also actually ask them.
* What do you like about yourself? Come on, you can do this!
* What kind of work do you do and how do you know you're good at it?

There is a deeply rooted connection between self-confidence/ esteem and accomplishing our goals. Take, for instance, people who enjoy gardening. Because having a nice garden is important to them, they take really good care of their gardens. They often enjoy showing other people their gardens with pride. This is how I would love for you to feel about yourself. When we believe that we are valuable and important, we take care of ourselves and make good decisions about our futures.

So many of us are willing to pour our emotional, physical, and spiritual energy into someone else or something else, such as gardening. Yet when it comes to setting goals for ourselves, we often change our minds, lose momentum, or simply give up. We tell ourselves that it's too hard, painful, or not worth it. This creates a vicious circle since what causes us to throw in the towel is low self-confidence and self-esteem. To gain these things, we need to feel accomplishment, dang it! Many people call these thoughts "limiting beliefs," but let's go ahead and reframe these ideas around our beliefs by discussing them as **encouraging and discouraging beliefs**.

We are going to spend a whole week on understanding your core beliefs and values, but let's touch on them briefly now because they greatly impact how we set goals for ourselves. Most of our beliefs are centered around our emotions, relationships, and goals. Check out this list of discouraging beliefs many of us have:

* I have no clue where to start.
* I can't afford this.
* I don't have time for this.
* I'm a procrastinator.
* I should have more motivation.
* I'm so fat/ugly/dumb.
* I should have more money.
* It's too late for me to change.
* What will people think if I do this?
* I don't deserve this.
* Why try? I'll only fail.

These discouraging beliefs become part of us, controlling our actions, behavior, and potential. We become who we believe we are. We may be intelligent, but if we skip studying and fail one test, we believe we are unintelligent from then on. We filter outside information in a way that confirms these negative beliefs, shaping our realities and our futures. We begin to adopt irrational thought patterns and develop a lack of motivation, which impacts our ability to set realistic goals.

But what if, instead of giving all of our mental space to discouraging beliefs, we started to consider what the future might look like if our biggest problems were solved?

YOUR VERY OWN CRYSTAL BALL!

The miracle question is a well-known exercise used in Solution-Focused Brief Therapy (SFBT). We're going to consider what your future looks like when a big problem in your life no longer exists. The idea here is to allow yourself to think of a huge range of possibilities instead of focusing on your same problems in the same ways. This is a two-phase process. If you can't come up with some kind of specific, well-formed goal right now, don't worry—that's not the purpose of this exercise. I only want you to start thinking about what is possible in your life.

THE MIRACLE QUESTION

What if you woke up tomorrow and a miracle had happened? The problem that has been plaguing you has been resolved. It's completely gone! Not only is this one problem gone, but many other aspects of your life have also improved because of it. Take a moment to consider this. And now tell me ... how do you see your life changing once your problem is gone? What will be different? How do you feel when you wake up? How would the people closest to you respond? Would they notice that you/your life seems different? Would they say it was better? And once this problem is gone, you have an exciting new question to consider: What will you do next? Grab your notebook and describe all of this in detail.

UNDERSTANDING WHAT YOU WANT

This is the yin and yang of self-esteem and self-confidence. When you feel good about yourself, you are likely to be more successful in all areas of your life. In order to achieve your goals, you also need to believe that you can learn, improve, and accomplish milestones that will take you where you want to go in these areas!

Some of the most common self-improvement goals we long to reach include: become more fit and healthy, develop more positivity in our lives, find our purpose, learn more skills to be successful, improve our personal relationships, and develop a deeper internal drive to challenge ourselves to learn new things. In order to achieve something that you start, you must be able to trust your abilities. Learning the simple techniques for goal setting I'm about to share will allow you to decide what success looks and feels like to you, and can help you move closer to the life you desire and deserve.

The techniques I've selected for this week can help improve many aspects of your daily life, but are *proven* to help you narrow down specific goals to improve your self-esteem and confidence.

These goals may include:
* I want to stop putting myself down.
* I want to stop comparing myself to others.
* I want to accept compliments graciously.
* I want to talk to myself kindly and with compassion.
* I want to stop drinking alcohol or using drugs.
* I want to communicate better.

My friend Tony's story can help us here. Remember how he described working with his therapist on *ways to improve how he accomplished things?* By starting small, he gained some clarity around *what he wanted from his life*, what *his dreams* were, and the *specific steps* he needed to take to reach them. His therapist helped him whittle down his goals to be *challenging yet doable*. Tony worked hard to change his internal mind-set, *trying out new techniques consistently* in order to see results. This was an excellent strategy! Let's give you the tools to follow it, too.

Tony's story laid out for us his short-, medium-, and long-term goals. Short-term goals are specific and are best scheduled every day, preferably at the same time so as to become routine. His short-term goal was to improve how he accomplished things and to find a therapist to work with him.

Medium-term goals are those that keep us interested and keep our soul-fire burning on the winding road to our destination. We can identify these types of goals through words like, "specific steps," and, "challenging yet doable."

Long-term goals often start as, "I want better self-confidence and self-esteem," or, "I want to feel better." These are simply too broad and hard to measure to actually reach. I encourage you to get more specific about your long-term outcome. For example, your goal could be elevating your self-confidence in social situations. Or it could be developing a consistent, positive self-image demonstrated by less negative self-talk and more assertiveness in communicating needs. My personal goal at the beginning of my journey was to establish an internal sense of acceptance and a sense of worthiness and competence. Goal setting is a primary tool that many mental health professionals use to support our clients' mental, physical, and emotional well-being. The confidence and self-esteem that comes with reaching goals assists people in moving forward in their lives, through stressful transitions and periods of anxiety, depression, and grief. An ever-important factor in developing your goals is your uniqueness. This is a collaborative effort because you have all the knowledge you need to accomplish your goals. My part is helping you become more aware of your individual needs and desires, and teaching you healthy ways to get them met. The following are three of the best ways to begin your personalized process by setting up your specific goals.

TECHNIQUE #1: GOALS FOR HOW WE CHANGE

Back in grad school, I was introduced to the researcher, John Norcross, who had been studying change, personal growth, and goal setting for many years. He defines a goal as "a mental representation of a desired outcome that a person is committed to." He and two of his friends—Carlo Di Clemente and James O. Prochaska—also developed a model of personal change based on the analysis of different theories of psychotherapy called The Transtheoretical Model (TTM), which studied how people quit smoking. They determined that people quit smoking more successfully if they were ready to do so, working on the assumption that people don't change their behaviors quickly or decisively. Instead, change occurs through a repetitive process by moving through different stages including contemplation, preparation, action, and maintenance. In order to progress through the stages of changing a behavior or a habit, they believe it best that we raise our awareness, experience relief, evaluate our progress, get feedback from others, find support, and substitute healthy behaviors and thoughts for unhealthy ones. Each of these can be accomplished through effective goal setting.

This week, we're going to do that by focusing on goal setting for the most common stages we see in therapy for self-esteem and self-confidence: **precontemplation and contemplation.**

THE PRECONTEMPLATION STAGE

In the **precontemplation stage**, many of us sit in painful silence, thinking about not having any control over our lives. We don't want to think about change. We may be resigned to living our life the way we are currently doing it. We might be in denial that change is possible for us or that we even need to change. Any of this sound familiar?

If you find yourself in this stage, allow yourself the opportunity to begin thinking about changing. You are working to motivate yourself and work toward acknowledging one or two long-term goals, by exploring your past, present, and future.

The Precontemplation (PPF) Questions:

✳ Past: Have you tried to change your self-esteem or confidence before?

✳ Present: What warning signs let you know that this is a problem?

✳ Future: What would have to happen for you to know that this is a significant problem?

The next stage is **contemplation,** where you begin weighing the costs and benefits of improving your self-esteem and self-confidence. Here, many of us express a slight desire to change but are subconsciously ruled by the "f" word: fear. Oftentimes, people will call me but don't leave a message to which I can respond. These folks are in contemplation. At this stage of the game, we tend to find ourselves working against our own resistance. We know we need some support and help, but it's very difficult to ask for it. It is in these moments that we gain either more clarity or create more barriers, so that's exactly what I will ask you to explore. Want to have a better idea of the benefits of initiating change and what is blocking you? You can set some short-term goals to assist you in removing those blocks.

The Contemplation Questions:

✳ Why do you want to change at this time?

✳ What are the reasons you don't want to change?

✳ What is keeping you from changing now?

✳ What has helped you in the past (people, programs, or behaviors) with improving your self-esteem and/or confidence?

✳ What would help you at this time?

✳ What do you think you need to learn about changing your behavior?

These two stages are truly about cultivating your awareness and commitment to developing goals that will help you change. I started with this technique so that you and I, along with others supporting you, can begin an ongoing conversation about lifestyle change and monitoring your willingness and readiness. These things are not static, so we must be open to expressing our ongoing desire, barriers, and reasons for changing or not. This will help ground you as you continue along your path toward lasting self-esteem.

Here is a tool you can use periodically to assess your readiness to change or keep changing:

The Readiness Ruler

On a scale of 0 to 10, with 0 being not ready at all and 10 being ready to change today or already changing, how ready are you to change your self-confidence and esteem?

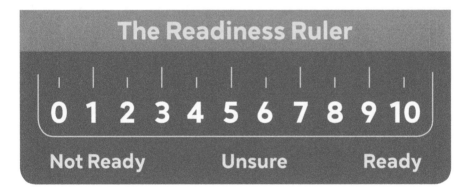

Follow up questions:

Why did you choose this number?

Why didn't you choose a lower number?

What would need to be different to move you to a higher number?

TECHNIQUE #2: GET YOUR WOOP ON!

During my research for this book, I came across a fabulous new evidence-based goal-setting technique which focuses on visualizing and writing out your wish, outcome, obstacles, and plan. The technique then focuses on building better self-esteem through changing your habits. Created by Gabriele Oettigen and Peter Gollwitzer, psychologists at New York University, and based on over 20 years of research, it has been proven to be effective in reducing insecurity-based behaviors across ages, cultures, and countries. Although I'm not a huge fan of acronyms, I'm jammin' on this one. Here is what WOOP stands for:

W – Wish: What's something you really want to accomplish? Something that makes you feel full of anticipation for the challenge ahead and the changes it could bring. Go ahead and pick something we can reasonably achieve over the five weeks we'll be working together. Try to summarize it in just a few words.

O – Outcome: Your wish comes true! What's the best possible outcome here? How would that make you feel?

O – Obstacle: Before your wish is granted, consider what could keep you from making that goal a reality. If you can, pick the one big thing that you can imagine getting in your way here. This could be anything from a bad habit—like procrastinating—to a deeply-felt emotion such as a belief that you're bound to fail.

P – Plan: Using an if/then way of thinking, write down how you'll tackle each obstacle. So, if X happens, then you'll do Y to overcome it!

Just in case you need an example, here is a WOOP plan for improving a personal relationship:

Wish: To be present with my partner.

Outcome: I will be in a more loving relationship and experience more joy and contentment.

Obstacle: I get distracted by my phone.

Plan: IF I'm going into a shared experience (a conversation, meal, bedtime, etc.), THEN I will put my phone on airplane mode and leave it in my bag or pocket across the room.

TECHNIQUE #3: SIMPLE SMART GOALS

For this technique, I am going to build on the idea of SMART goals. The acronym is believed to have gotten its start way back when George T. Doran used the term in the November 1981 issue of *Management Review*. Over the years, the letters in SMART have taken different meanings, but they've proven to be very effective for clarifying your ideas, focusing your efforts, and increasing your chances of reaching your goals. The process is very straightforward. This is the basic structure:

Specific (simple, sensible, significant)

Measurable (motivating, meaningful)

Achievable (attainable, actionable)

Relevant (realistic, results-driven)

Time-bound (timely, time-mindful)

Let's break these down further.

S – Specific: As you're getting used to hearing, broad goals can feel hard to measure and difficult to achieve. You'll do better by getting specific. If you need some help getting as specific as you need to be, try answering a W question below:

* Who will be involved?
* What do I want to accomplish?
* When do I want to accomplish this?
* Which resources or limitations are involved?
* Why is this goal important to me?

M – Measurable: Since we have a five-week period to work together, let's identify some ways we can mark off progress week-by-week. Consider what makes the most sense with the goals you've chosen. Perhaps you want to engage in less and less of a particular behavior each week. In that case, you may want to keep a small notebook with you to jot down a tally mark whenever you notice yourself engaging in that behavior. At the end of the week, tally up!

A – Achievable: What would make this goal attainable? Are there any tools you need before you get started? Do you have a support network in place? If there's anything you realize you need, come up with a plan for getting it.

R – Relevant: Consider if your goal is actually going to help you on your way to achieving everything you want out of life. If you want to become a skilled woodworker because having a final product you can be proud of would increase your confidence, great! But if you want to become a skilled woodworker because you think it sounds cool, it might be good to reconsider. What would actually make you feel like you're moving forward on your own path?

T – Time-Bound: Give yourself a time frame to work within. While I recommend picking something you think you can accomplish in five weeks, you may find the real goal you want to achieve will take several months. If that's the case, pick a reasonable milestone you could reach by the time you complete this book.

WRITING YOUR SMART GOALS

To get you started, here is an example of a SMART goal for self-confidence:

Initial Goal: I want to improve my self-confidence and self-esteem

S: I want to challenge my negative self-talk.

M: I will measure and document my progress by counting the number of negative statements I make one day a week.

A: I will achieve this by paying attention to my subconscious thinking and by practicing self-awareness of my negative thoughts.

R: I want to reduce my negative thinking and apply the same compassion I give others to myself.

T: I will accomplish this in nine months.

Now it's your turn! I recommend setting at least three goals for developing your self-confidence and self-esteem. Let's turn the page and get started.

S.M.A.R.T GOALS WORKSHEET

INITIAL GOAL	WRITE THE GOAL YOU HAVE IN MIND
S SPECIFIC	What do you want to accomplish? Who needs to be included? When do you want to do this? Why is this a goal?
M MEASURABLE	How can you measure progress and know if you've successfully met your goals?
A ACHIEVABLE	Do you have the skills required to achieve the goal? If not, can you obtain them? What is the motivation for this goal? Is the amount of effort required on par with what the goal will achieve?
R RELEVANT	Why am I setting this goal now? Is it aligned with my overall objectives?
T TIME-BOUND	What's the deadline and is it realistic?
SMART GOAL	Review what you have written, and craft a new goal statement based on what the answers to the questions above have revealed.

Journaling

Writing in a journal is a fantastic way to learn more about yourself. You can write in sentences, fragments, or thoughts; the form doesn't matter as much as the consistent practice. Journaling has long been a basic and effective tool for self-growth. Moving forward, each week I will spotlight a morning and evening activity. The morning activity will be a journal prompt focusing on the topic of the week. I'll mix it up for the evening activities.

If you haven't yet designated a notebook for working through this book, you may want to go get one now.
Journal Prompts:

1. I believe I can _____ because _____.

2. I need _____ today because _____.

3. What do you do and say to yourself when something does not work out as planned?

4. How can you be gentle and forgiving with yourself today?

5. Describe your biggest fear when it comes to accomplishing your dream goal.

6. Who inspires you and why?

Do you want to make your SMART goals even smarter? Write down a graduated series of goals for your **initial goal**.

Let's take your initial goal and extend it into the future by creating new goals that build directly off it. Consider the following questions:

Once I've accomplished my initial goal, what will I do in the following weeks? What will my next goal(s) be? We'll call these your short-term goals.

How about in the next few months? If I accomplish all my short-term goals, where do I want to go and how do I want to grow from there? Those are your medium-term goals. *As I imagine accomplishing all of these goals—what will it feel like to consider the next few years? What do I want to accomplish in the years to come?* These will be your long-term goals.

SETTING ACHIEVABLE GOALS

I'd like to share my own personal story around learning to set realistic goals. For most of my life, I have set very high goals which I sometimes achieve. You see, I'm really good at the big, flashy, dance-on-the-table stuff. But I didn't have the skills to embrace a daily routine that would help me live a more peaceful life. Ultimately, in order to maintain my self-confidence, I had to keep setting my sights on bigger and bigger successes. I thought that was the only way to be loved and appreciated. What I didn't know was that I was creating a life that was not sustainable. Moving from one shiny object to another, I began daily practices of self-loathing.

In 2008, I decided to leave my marriage, but I was not quite ready to undertake any true personal change, much less explore realistic goal setting. My lack of desire to change only led me to drastically increase the only coping skill I had: drinking wine. Luckily for me, I finally grew way too tired to keep this façade going. I went to residential treatment for my overuse of alcohol, attended therapy, and got involved with a like-minded community of my counselors and sober peeps, and they immediately introduced me to the stages of change. Sure enough, even while at residential treatment for addiction, I was still in the early stage of contemplation. I worked with some excellent counselors who helped me with the process of developing attainable goals. They encouraged me to take small steps and celebrate all my mini-successes. I am eternally grateful for the many goals I have achieved over the last nine years and will continue to practice my own special way of setting goals.

WHERE ARE YOU ON THE WHEEL OF LIFE? THE ART PROJECT THAT'S SECRETLY A QUIZ

Where are all these goals going to get you anyway? What good is a goal if it isn't helping you grow in some way? The Wheel of Life—originally created by Paul Meyer, creator of Success Motivation Institute and one of the originators of what has become known as "life coaching"—is a simple yet profound way of taking a look at how balanced your life is. This tool will help you visualize how well you're functioning in eight different areas of your life.

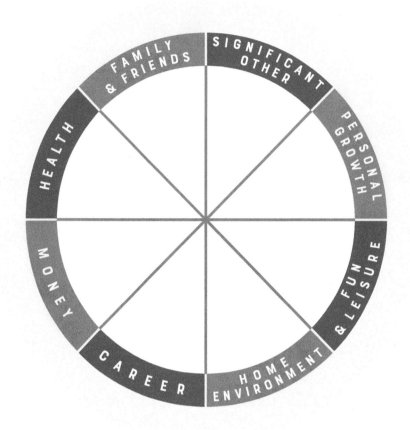

Instructions:

1. Copy your own Wheel of Life in your notebook. Don't worry if it isn't a perfect circle or things wind up looking a bit uneven—the important part is to have all the categories there. If there are any categories that don't feel relevant to you, create categories of your own!

2. Have the center of each wedge represent a zero—meaning you have no satisfaction in that area—and the outer edge of the wedge represent a 10: perfect satisfaction. Color in each wedge to your current satisfaction levels.

3. Once you've got everything colored, let's take a look at it:

 ✳ Which wedge or wedges were the biggest surprise for you?

 ✳ Write down a couple sentences under your wheel about how
   this exercise made you feel. What are your big takeaways?

 ✳ Pick one wedge that's looking a little dismal to you and consider
   what would bring it up to a 10. What would a 10 even look like
   to you in this category?

BODY, HEALTH, AND MENTAL WELLNESS

Like many of us, I loved to indulge myself in what I believed to be
self-care. I would schedule regular massages, facials, manicures, and
pedicures. My most important self-care reward was a glass of wine
(or four) after working out, working hard, or at the end of any given
day. To me, doing these things was strong evidence that I was taking
very good care of myself, proving that I set aside time for my well-
being. But those methods did not truly soothe my stress, anxiety, and
internal discomfort, no matter how much I wanted to believe they did.

Effective self-care is about supporting our needs. Back then, I did
not realize what my needs were, much less feel as if I was worthy of
getting them met. That's why I needed weekly massages and turned
to distracting myself with exercise and numbing myself with alcohol.
Those of us who experience low self-confidence and self-esteem
tend to avoid things that actually are proven to improve and sustain
our mental and physical wellness, such as time alone, inner reflection,
and therapy. We often opt instead to seek comfort through external
validation alongside unhealthy coping skills such as over-using
substances, people-pleasing, and busyness.

There is a strong correlation between low self-esteem and
struggling to include self-care practices into our lifestyle choices.
Oftentimes, this lack of self-nurturing leads to sadness, anxiety,
and low motivation. Practicing a healthy ritual of self-care is often
second-guessed as selfishness. We tend to prioritize everything and
everyone else before ourselves. We become overworked, overtired,

and overstressed because we are overdoing it. To become more balanced and self-assured, we need to stop ignoring our needs and begin placing our well-being higher on our "to-do" lists.

Setting up a routine of daily self-care based on my needs and immediate goals for my well-being has made a significant difference in my ability to meet my long-term life goals. The following is a list of self-care tips that you can choose from to practice over the next few weeks. Choose no more than three so as not to overwhelm yourself or the people around you! The important thing here is to practice self-care that is meaningful to you on a daily basis and develop a better relationship with that person you have been ignoring: you.

* Get some fresh air.
* Treat yourself to a nourishing and sumptuous meal, alone.
* Escape with a book.
* Rock out to your favorite music.
* Do something childlike and whimsical.
* Put your phone away for a designated amount of time.
* Laugh from your belly.
* Color in a coloring book
* Go swing in your hammock, sit on your outdoor furniture, or lay on the grass.
* Spend time with an animal or pet.
* Find something beautiful and look at it for a while.
* Take a nap during the day.
* Massage your feet and/or hands.
* Give yourself a hug or hold your own hand. (Yeah, my clients roll their eyes at this one, too.)
* Have a good cry.
* Say something nice to yourself and then repeat it aloud.
* Remove one task from your to-do list.
* Light a candle and watch it flicker.
* Ask for help.
* Listen for the quiet voice inside you; that's your intuition.

A wise mentor shared with me the difference between the words "routine" and "practice." She taught me how it affected her ability to set and keep daily goals for her self-care. She showed me the value of my words and how they impact my subconscious motivation. Morning routines are drudgery for many of us—we perceive them to be a rushed sequence of actions. It becomes a drill and a chore. My friend invited me to rethink my routine, instead turning what I do throughout my day into a practice. A practice is doing something in order to get better at it. Mind blown! We need both routine and practice in our lives. Routines are good because we don't have to think about them. Practices inspire more meaning and a deeper commitment. I personally like the word "practice" better because it gives me a feeling of living on purpose.

Declare a Commitment

Research tells us that not just making a goal, but telling someone what the goal is (even if it's just out loud to ourself), makes us more likely to follow through with it. Take a minute to write down a goal you focused on in this chapter.

Now say it out loud to yourself or to at least one other person. Say it loud and proud!

As we move into Week Two, consider these questions: *What did I learn this week? What skills, information, or stories resonated with me? How do I feel about moving forward?*

You may want to take a minute to jot down some reflections in your notebook so you can refer back to your major takeaways whenever you want to set a new goal.

CHAPTER 4
Week Two - Meeting and Confronting Your Inner Critic

This week, we are going to:

* Explore your inner critic;

* Learn how to catch your critic in the act;

* Develop a practice of calling out your critic; and

* Find ways to live with your critic.

We'll build on:

* The goals you have set;

* Your strengths, motivation, and readiness; and

* Your self-improvement priorities.

When is the last time you woke up in the morning expressing love and appreciation to yourself? Like, "Hey, Lynn! You are so good at what you do, you make such good decisions, and wow, you are hot!" It usually doesn't go that way, right? It often sounds more like, "Why didn't you get that done? You are so bad at that and nobody likes you."

Last week was all about discovering your motivations, strengths, and the areas in which you want to see improvement in your confidence and esteem in the next few weeks, months, or even years. But many of us experience a block that often derails our efforts: our inner critic. In week two, we're going to learn more about your personal inner critic, catch it in the act, have a little chat about what its up to, and discuss some necessary boundaries for a peaceful, long-term relationship.

Ellie, a smart and funny woman in her mid 30s, came to see me to discuss her increasing anxiety about her future. She was very down on herself and losing sleep worrying about the fact that she was not yet married and had no children, but very much wanted to have a family. I asked her to tell me some of the things she was saying to herself, especially when she was trying to fall asleep. She replied that although she couldn't remember the exact words, it seemed to revolve around how many of her friends were married with kids and that her older sister was "always in [her] head."

Ellie had long looked up to and compared herself to her sister, often finding herself coming up short. This left her with a heavy feeling of unworthiness. Over the years, these feelings caused many problems between them. When they spoke or got together, Ellie felt her sister bragged and offered up not-so-subtle criticisms, sometimes going so far as saying that Ellie was "not doing the right thing or just being stupid." Mostly, Ellie silently nodded in agreement with her sister.

Having internalized all this criticism since childhood, Ellie had adopted a pattern of being her own worst critic. Her thoughts revolved around what she was not accomplishing in life as opposed to some of the wonderful things she already had accomplished. She loved being a theater director. She loved building unity within the production by exploring the different elements of writing, directing, staging, costumes, lighting, and sound. Her dream was to win a Tony award, and she was already very respected and sought-after in the industry. Ellie loved traveling around the country and the world, and enjoying the many creative relationships her job offered her.

Together, we worked on building compassion and exploring the severely critical inner voice she was paying attention to and believing. She began to recognize how hurtful it was to compare herself to her sister, and to understand that they were good at different things and had different desires. Ellie began to build awareness of her inner critic and found ways of coping that fit her lifestyle. Over time, she began to uncover her needs, values, and dreams. She accepted and committed to her very own choices and path in life.

WHO IS MY INNER CRITIC?

Your inner critic is a devious little being who capitalizes on discomfort, fear, and stress. Your critical inner voice carries on a running, mostly subconscious, monologue of judgment and personal attacks. It is most active when you want to take a risk or step outside your normal routine and comfort zone. It uses extremely powerful words, ones that have deep and distinctive meaning in your life. Many of us assume that these thoughts are accurate simply because we're thinking them.

Your inner critic is masterful at repetitive rumination, keeping you stuck in regrets, judgments, blaming, and catastrophizing. A 2015 study by J. Paul Hamilton and colleagues gave us a peek into what may be happening in our brains when we go down the rabbit hole of depressive and repetitive rumination. They found our default mode network (DMN) is engaged when we self-reflect, daydream, or reminisce—that natural state our minds create for restful wandering. The prefrontal cortex helps guide the DMN to take advantage of our reflections toward gentle and effective problem solving. When the inner critic takes over, it hijacks our healthy self-reflection, turning our daydreaming into a repeating spiral of negativity.

I want to make a distinction here between your mind and your brain. Your brain is a physical organ, often associated with the mind and consciousness. But our minds are not confined to our brain matter or even our skulls. Our mind flows to every cell in our body, and has significant and impressive control over our internal body systems. The brain is tangible; we can see it, and trained surgeons can sometimes fix it if it is injured or damaged. Our minds are energetic and ethereal manifestations of thoughts, feelings, attitudes, beliefs, and imagination.

Those of us in the field of psychology tend to concentrate on human thinking as an intellectual process connecting the mind with the brain. Our goal could be to solve a problem, answer a question, or learn a new skill. Although many tend to focus on negative self-talk, our internal monologue is also made up of positive self-talk. Both of these play a vital role in our mental health. When we speak positively to ourselves, it's helpful! We tend to be present in the moment, see the reality of what's happening, and use healthier ways of dealing with underlying beliefs and biases. However, those moments are far too short and infrequent for most of us.

There is a disturbing trend happening in which "thought leaders" and social media influencers are using mantras and "empowering" words in an attempt to build self-confidence. In some cases, they claim it will improve our self-esteem. This movement oversimplifies and distorts the nature of our beautiful human complexity. The idea that proclaiming we are a "badass" or "boss" or simply shifting our mind-set by expelling our limiting beliefs is not realistic. This surface mind-set shift may offer some subtle movement in your conscious problematic thoughts, but the unconscious has more control over us, and a stronger, more unhealthy critical voice.

Instead, I believe paying closer attention to our thought process around issues of self-image or during times of self-reflection can help us tap into our subconscious sense of self. That's when we tend to learn the key to unlocking our personal pathway to better self-esteem and confidence.

I love to practice CBT to understand the way we use memory and language to make decisions. We can observe and learn our pattern of processing internal self-talk. There is much speculation about how many thoughts we have per day, with estimates ranging from 12 to 60 thousand. There's an even wider estimation about how many of those thoughts are negative: anywhere between 20 and 80 percent.

Our inner critic is negative for a reason. It evolved from our earliest ancestors' need to remain physically safe. However, this basic need for protection in the physical world does not translate well to protection in our world of mental well-being. The modern inner critic has turned its focus inward in an attempt to keep us from internal pain. Unfortunately, it is really quite bad at this.

Charles Fernyhough, a professor at Durham University in the UK and author of the book *The Voices Within*, teaches a theory that our inner monologue develops right alongside our ability to speak. This theory emerged in the 1920s when a Russian psychologist named Lev Vygotsky stated that children learn and develop by forming a partnership with their parents. The parent or caregiver speaks and shows how to master a skill or task. The child then goes off on their own, often speaking aloud in the parents' voice as they repeat and practice the skill or task. Over time, this "self-talk" becomes increasingly more silent and internalized. What was first a dialogue with your parents has now become your internal monologue.

I am an avid people watcher by nature and profession, and I find it fascinating to observe the development of social dialogue and private speech in children. As children, we are rarely taught the many "feeling" words used to translate and communicate our internal world to others. We all can learn a great deal by simply observing a child playing. Consider one of my young clients, a six-year-old boy who had been acting out at school and was being labeled a bully. At the beginning of our first session, he was quiet and looked somewhat afraid, as though he might be in trouble. I took him to a bigger room with pillows and asked him to play with the toys that he'd brought along, his favorites. Out of his bag came several action figures with menacing faces. He set up a fortress and immediately began creating what can only be called a siege. "Watch out, the bad guys are going to get you," he said, as he rammed through one of the pillows and into the fortress. "See, I can get you, now you're bad, too," he said in a louder voice to the dolls inside the fortress. This became a pattern during our sessions, and I learned that he felt pretty helpless and fearful overall. The language he continued to use was aggressively demanding: "No, stop that!" and, "You should know better!" He hadn't yet learned how to express feelings, so he was left to express his pain and fear through his behavior, his play.

So far, we have discussed two types of self-talk which are diametrically opposed: positive and negative. But some of our daily chatter is much more ordinary and reasonable. Thoughts such as, *I wish I had some peanut butter* or *I'll share that with her when she wakes up* are examples of common, everyday self-talk. This is the third type of self-talk: *neutral.*

The fourth and last type of self-talk is called *instructional*, when our inner voice guides us through a specific task. From these types, we can discern that there are different purposes for our internal monologue. Talking to ourselves both silently and out loud can help us plan, organize, motivate, and analyze, but it can also reprimand and punish us.

Our negative thoughts are absolutely optional, yet with all of the healthy and realistic ways of thinking available to us, we still tend to focus on that one category. This book is going to help you think on purpose—to choose what to think and when. Instead of thinking on autopilot and unconsciously reacting to our world, we can practice the art of choosing ahead of time how we want our brain to process people, places, and things.

Why do so many of us struggle with our negative self-talk? It's the big "f" word: *fear*. Humans (along with most other species) feel fear in order to keep us safe from anything we deem threatening. Humanity originally developed an internal safety system to alert us that we needed to defend ourselves by engaging one of four basic defense tactics: fighting (facing the threat), fleeing (running from the threat), freezing (playing dead), or submitting (going belly up, like a puppy). Our early ancestors found these defenses quite useful, allowing them to stay alive in an extremely dangerous environment and to survive long enough to procreate, which kept our species evolving. However, today these strategies and their responses often cause us great confusion and negatively impact our mental well-being. The threats are often no longer against our lives. Our threats come in the form of stressors which tend to be perceived as attacks against self-image or our purpose in the world. As our stress levels increase, the areas of our brain which are in charge of protecting us take over. In a sense, we "devolve," and our bodies flood with adrenaline, cortisol, and dopamine as a means of coping with the possibility of our demise.

Understanding all of this helped me to accept that my negative inner voice is actually trying to help me. The problem is that we have not yet learned how to consistently reprogram our thought process. Most of us don't even question the way we think and are unaware that there are effective ways of changing our thought patterns and the very structure of our brains. It is my opinion that we are currently undertaking that part of our evolution as humans. We are addressing how we perceive stress. One way we can do this is by getting curious and learning how our inner critic works against us, but also for us. Let's start by learning about how your inner critic is actually trying to protect you.

STONE AGE VERSUS MODERN AGE: THE EFFECTS OF THE STRESS RESPONSE

In this exercise, let's explore the differences between how stone age and modern age people benefited from their body's response to stressors. Ask yourself this:

THE FIGHT RESPONSE

What do I want to do when I get stressed? Do I want to punch the wall? Then you're experiencing the **fight response**: Our bodies prepare for physical activity by releasing adrenaline, increasing heart rate, speeding up breathing, and tensing muscles. We lose the ability to focus, and our sensitivity toward danger is heightened.

Stone Age: They took an aggressive physical stance with a desire to stay alive.

Modern Age: We take the fight internal, beating ourselves up with cruel language.

THE FLIGHT RESPONSE

Do I want to run? Then you're experiencing the **flight response:**
Our bodies prepare to run by releasing adrenaline, increasing heart
rate, speeding up breathing, and tensing muscles as in fight, but our
thinking becomes quicker and our attention is sharpened toward
finding escape routes.

Stone Age: They weighed the cost of staying and fighting versus
fleeing in order to save their lives or the lives of others.

Modern Age: We become anxious, uncomfortable, and discontent,
often fleeing from ourselves using substances or other distractions
to numb these feelings.

THE FREEZE RESPONSE

Am I unable to think or move? Then you're experiencing the **freeze
response:** Our bodies quickly cycle through a brief and intense need
to escape, then our emotions become numb. We are slow or unable
to move and may experience an "out of body" feeling.

Stone Age: They would "play dead" in order to trick the large, wild
creatures into moving on to other prey.

Modern Age: We spend hours stuck in rumination, thinking about
what we did wrong in the past or how we might fail in the future.

THE SUBMIT/APPEASE RESPONSE

Do I want to shrink? Then you're experiencing the **submit/appease
response:** We focus on options that might reduce the immediate
threat and may adopt a submissive body posture, making ourselves
smaller and averting our gaze.

Stone Age: They would crouch and show passivity with the hope
that the threat would move on.

Modern Age: We avoid conflict by agreeing and placating. We often experience regret and resentment afterwards, turning our harsh judgment inward and blaming ourselves.

See how all that stress is influencing you? It's no wonder, then, that such a high proportion of our self-talk is so negative and that it can feel inescapable.

TYPES OF INNER CRITIC

As most of us know, negative self-talk can be extremely toxic. Studies have indicated that the most common effects of listening to and believing our inner critic are:

* Feelings of anxiety and depression.
* Problems in relationships, especially around conflict.
* Lack of motivation and "caged" thinking resulting from the belief that you can't do something.
* Perfectionism—great is not good enough.

It turns out that our inner critic is one of the most difficult and persistent mental wellness issues we all face. Importantly, our inner critic also has multiple personalities. Most of us have a number of self-judging critic-protectors all with different motivations for existing. Jay Earley, PhD, and Bonnie Weiss, LCSW, have studied and written about the inner critic and identified the seven types that most of us struggle with. Assess yourself by taking a look at the list on the next page and identifying the top three types that make up your inner critic.

PERFECTIONIST

The Perfectionist is, at heart, trying to protect you from rejection. A great way to do that (or so it thinks) is to never make a mistake. If you're an artist, and you don't like the way your latest painting is shaping up, there's no use in seeing what other direction that particular piece might go—throw it out and start over, the Perfectionist demands. This inner voice probably learned how to talk this way from someone important to you. If you listen carefully, you may be able to identify who that voice truly belongs to. Living under the "never good enough" standards of a Perfectionist can feel like a major blow to your confidence and esteem.

The Perfectionist usually says:

* ✳ *Try harder!*
* ✳ *You will never do it right.*
* ✳ *You're not planning to leave it like that, are you?*
* ✳ *Your work is worthless!*

INNER CONTROLLER

The Inner Controller cannot abide by setbacks. *If you've failed at your diet once before,* says the Inner Controller, *then you'll fail again.* And it is very disappointed in and angry at you. At times, it might feel like the Inner Controller is really trying to harness your best urges, but it does this by trying (and failing) to strangle your worst ones, especially as they relate to things like eating, drinking, and sex. It can be hard to try to build up a good foundation of esteem and confidence with the Inner Controller constantly wagging its finger at you.

The Inner Controller usually says:

* ✳ *You did it again . . . shame on you!*
* ✳ *You have no willpower.*
* ✳ *You will never break free from this!*

TASKMASTER

Work, work, and work some more, and when you're finally done, you can reward yourself by working on something else. The Taskmaster wants you to be successful, but its tactics and expectations can be awfully unreasonable. And if it keeps grinding at that grindstone, it's bound to achieve exactly the opposite of what it wants: You'll fight back by putting off doing what needs to be done. And with that push-pull of the Taskmaster telling you to work more and work harder, and the procrastinator it can awaken within, it may start to feel impossible to ever feel good about yourself and your accomplishments.

The Taskmaster usually says:

* *You're lazy.*
* *Get to work already!*
* *Rest is for the weak.*
* *You won't achieve anything in life unless you start working harder.*

UNDERMINER

The Underminer would really rather you never leave the safety of your own home—after all, you'll never encounter failure if you just never try! And it's willing to play dirty to get what it wants. Though the Underminer wants you to stay safe, it also wants you to stay small. It takes direct shots at your confidence and esteem to ensure you never feel good enough about yourself to try to accomplish, well, anything.

The Underminder usually says:

* *Don't even try because you will fail anyway.*
* *It's pointless.*
* *Why waste time on this?*

DESTROYER

You know how you could stay safest of all? By never having existed in the first place. If that sounds brutal, then you won't be surprised to learn this inner critic's name is Destroyer. It pulverizes every shred of confidence, esteem, and even feelings of basic worth that you have. The Destroyer doesn't just want you to think you're not worth anything—it wants you to think that everyone else thinks that, too. Many Destroyers are born from terrible circumstances early in life. If you ever feel like there's something fundamentally wrong about taking up space in the world, then you may have a Destroyer on your hands.

The Destroyer usually says:

* *You should have never been born.*
* *You are one big failure.*
* *You are worthless.*

GUILT-TRIPPER

If you're familiar with lying in bed at night and replaying that one mean thing you once said to someone back in middle school over and over again, like the worst movie of all time showing on your mind's theater nonstop, then you've met the Guilt-Tripper. Did you once make a mistake? Go against the grain to poor results? The Guilt-Tripper will never, *ever* let you forget it. It may think it's protecting you from making mistakes again, but all its really doing is stomping on your confidence and esteem.

The Guilt-Tripper usually says:

* *How could you do this?*
* *You will regret this for the rest of your life.*
* *They will never forgive you.*
* *You will never forgive yourself.*

You know what would be great? If everyone liked you all the time! And hey, the Conformist has a great plan for how to accomplish this: Never disagree with anyone. Your family wants you to keep attending a church you no longer feel at home in? The Conformist pushes you to stay. Feel like you've got an inner self just waiting to break free? The Conformist would rather that didn't happen. Because what if someone didn't like it? The Conformist wants you to be accepted, which we all want to some extent. But the Conformist would strictly hold you in a life you don't really want—never allowing you to develop confidence or esteem in your true self— to achieve that.

The Conformist usually says:

* *Don't make a fool of yourself.*
* *Keep your head down!*
* *Do as you are told.*
* *What will people think?*

We all have some mix of these inner critics living inside us, fighting us for control of self-esteem and confidence. Let's learn how to fight back.

AWARENESS AND CATCHING THE CRITIC IN THE ACT

What is self-awareness? I love a definition by psychologists Shelley Duval and Robert Wicklund, who were integral in the development of the theory of self-awareness. They state, "When we focus our attention on ourselves, we evaluate and compare our current behavior to our internal standards and values. We become self-conscious as an objective evaluator of ourselves." That's a bunch of goodness! I encourage building a better relationship with yourself.

Using awareness is the first step toward improving your relationship with yourself. The first challenge is to take note of how often your negative inner voice reveals itself in everyday life. Oftentimes, we don't even acknowledge what we are thinking in the moment. Have you ever found yourself exhausted at the end of the day and can't figure out why? It may be because this critical voice has been operating just on the outskirts of your consciousness and wearing you down. According to a study published and led by associate professor of psychology, Ezequiel Morsella of San Francisco State University, it's our subconscious that is in charge most of the time. In order to challenge these undetected, havoc-creating thoughts, we must learn to acknowledge them for what they are: simply thoughts.

This was an important revelation for me as I embarked on my personal development journey. What a comfort it was to know that the thoughts (accompanied by feelings) showing up in my head did not define me. I was not the voice speaking—I was the person hearing it. My negative internal voice was a constant source of worry and angst, causing me to be in a perpetual state of fight, flight, freeze, or submission. She would show up in a variety of places: When I met new people, dealt with challenging people, met with my boss, when I had to do something I didn't want to do, and, of course, when I was alone. The voice I call "Nasty Nelly" would say things like, "Don't say anything dumb," or, "You're stupid." Sometimes it would tell me, "You're not attractive," or, "You don't deserve this," or, "You aren't like other people." Any of those sound familiar for you?

While many of us know this critic exists, we rarely challenge the voice inside of us as inaccurate. As I mentioned earlier, the first step is to commit to catching your critic in the act. You can learn to listen on purpose and take note of words such as "failure," "should," "idiot," "imposter," "liar," and "never." By slowing down and allowing time and energy for self-reflection, you can notice more of what you don't like about what your voice is saying.

> ## Transcribing Your Critic
>
> Keep a notebook at your bedside. As you reflect on your day before you fall asleep, write down the negative words your inner critic is saying to you. It may also be helpful to write one or two words about the situation for which you are punishing yourself.

CALLING OUT THE CRITIC

Our inner critic does not want us to notice it. Why? Because it thinks we cannot take care of ourselves without its help. In an effort to help us, our critic works mostly behind a curtain of sorts, and works hard to make sure we follow its rules. Day after day, the critic undermines our intuition and attacks, exaggerates, and blames, leading to low self-worth and low self-esteem. As Michael Corleone said in *The Godfather*, "Keep your friends close and your enemies closer." We can definitely use our closeness with our inner critic to our advantage.

In an effort to get to know our inner critic better, we need to uncover and clarify any ulterior motive, no matter how well-intentioned, so we can expose its true motivation.

TECHNIQUE #1: IDENTIFY

Fold a piece of blank paper in half. Take a few moments to think about any of the negative things you've been telling yourself in the last few days. Write those down on the left side. Take your time and be sure to list at least three to five of them. Now, translate each of them into the second person. For example, if you said, "I've been so lazy," (my personal favorite), you will write, "You've been so lazy." Write these statements on the right side of the page, then read them out loud. Notice your tone of voice. Is it sarcastic or mean? How does it feel when you hear this out loud in your own voice?

TECHNIQUE #2: NAME AND SEPARATE YOUR INNER CRITIC

This is such a fun one! In order to acknowledge that your inner critic is not yourself, it's helpful to give it a name. Mine is called Nasty or Negative Nelly, and she sits on my shoulder. I don't see her as a part of my personality, only someone who is attempting to influence me. She is the culmination of other people's criticisms of me and all the feelings and needs I've internalized over the years. She hides behind words like "should" and "can't." I don't like her or her company, so I acknowledge her for who she is and call her out! Silliness, fun, and levity are encouraged when deciding on a name for your inner critical voice.

Now that this mean voice has a name, let's write out some ways to separate you from your inner critic. Feel free to say these directly to whatever little creature you are using to represent your inner critic. Here are some examples for you to follow:

* *Nelly, I don't like you criticizing me. Go away!*
* *Nelly, stop comparing me to others in the hope that I find someone who is less than me and makes me feel better about myself!*
* *Nelly, I get that you want me to be perfect in all that I do so I feel safe, but your way is not working!*
* *Nelly, stop putting me down in an effort to make amends for what I've done wrong—it's a bad idea!*

TECHNIQUE #3: UNTANGLING FROM YOUR CRITIC

Once you name and separate from your inner critic, it will be possible to have a true dialogue with it. Using ACT, we can address our inner critic by accepting it for what it is rather than analyzing it or wanting it to go away. Then you can commit to doing something about it. You can decide to learn a new way of coping with your fears, and not let your cave-person stress responses take over.

A technique called diffusion allows us to separate ourselves from our thoughts and lessen the negative impact they have on our behavior. It's a type of detaching with love.

First, you'll need to identify two specific thoughts you would like to untangle yourself from. Take a moment to consider the impact that holding on to each thought has had on your life. This could be a resentment, a regret about your past, or a negative prediction about your future. Next, consider a much more compassionate and meaningful response to yourself when this thought appears. It's okay to acknowledge any uncomfortable feelings you may have in order to make room for a more helpful statement.

Example: Instead of thinking, "I'm never going to be happy," say to yourself, "I am having a thought that I'm never going to be happy."

The purpose of this exercise is to support the notion that thoughts are just thoughts; they are only mental events, not facts. We are simply learning to notice our thoughts, watch them, accept them, and let them go when we are ready.

TECHNIQUE #4: LOSE THE FILTERS

The most effective CBT techniques that we apply in therapy are based on what we called *cognitive distortions* or *distorted thinking*. They are so very important to our process of working with your inner critic because these are filters that our inner critic applies to trick us into believing that what it is saying is true and factual. By learning to recognize when you are thinking distorted thoughts, you begin to question such thoughts, with the hope of then replacing them with more balanced ones. This might sound simple, but distorted negative thinking is often unconscious and can be seen as "normal" to you. Changing these self-defeating thoughts into a healthier, balanced way of thinking can be quite a process. But it's not impossible. This is truly a case of "practice makes perfect." Here's how you can start:

Ever find yourself wondering out loud where the heck your keys are or what time that meeting is with your boss? Making your internal voice external in these cases is actually very healthy. Keep in mind we are not talking about your negative inner critic here. This is when we feel some stress or anxiety and need some confirmation. When we speak out loud, it helps us slow our thoughts down and process them differently, because we're engaging with the language centers of our brain. It's a good thing.

Asking ourselves out loud where our keys are helps us visualize where we usually put them and find them sooner! It's sort of like a spoken journal that walks us through our lives in real time. One strong argument I make to my clients is that if you talk to yourself out loud, you are better able to catch when your inner critic is being mean. In these cases, you can check yourself, taking advantage of what you hear. This can allow you to more positively work through difficult emotions such as anger, sadness, and confusion. Several studies have even indicated that asking yourself questions out loud while studying something has significantly improved learning. Why don't you give it a whirl? Talk to yourself out loud!

LIVING WITH THE CRITIC

It is my hope that you now have a better understanding of this critical self that lives inside of you, and that you are moving from believing all that negativity into a sort of love-hate relationship. If this is where you're at, it is possible to make friends and embrace your personal inner critic. After all, your critic isn't going anywhere—it is a part of you and you need it. The very best way I have discovered to live with my Negative Nelly is to be kind to her and show her compassion.

It's pretty hard to stop and say something kind to someone who is attacking you, using your vulnerabilities and insecurities as sharp and prodding weapons. But the research in this area is recent and strong. Compassion is where it's at when it comes to that nasty voice from within. Professor and author Dr. Kristen Neff, along with many other notables in the field of the psychology of self-confidence and self-esteem, suggests that recognizing our own humanity as we would someone else's, along with being kind and compassionate with ourselves, will earn us the biggest payoff in our self-esteem and self-love.

Here and Now

Find yourself a quiet spot. Take a few deep breaths and think of a situation that's causing you difficulty. See if you can feel the emotional distress and discomfort in your body. Now, say to yourself: *That hurts.*

Next, acknowledge that you are human by saying: *Other people feel this way, too.*

Follow this by saying: *May I learn to accept myself for who I am. May I be patient and learn to forgive myself.*

STARTING TO THINK DIFFERENTLY

Starting is half the battle. If you've read this far, pat yourself on the back, because you are on your way to better self-confidence! Our internal lives have a great impact on our emotional well-being and our self-esteem. The more we are aware of its impact, the greater our ability to live in harmony with it. When we live on autopilot, accepting our thoughts as real and factual, we turn away from awareness and curiosity. Autopilot is easier, but it's unsustainable and doesn't protect us from self-doubt and pain.

Lasting change is not about the destination. By adopting the idea of lifelong learning and focusing on the daily process of curiosity and practice, we can take advantage of our small everyday victories, which will build our self-confidence. What if you improved your ability to catch your inner critic in the act 1 percent more each day this week? Would you be better or worse off in the end? Let's find out by practicing to identify our negative thoughts.

The queen of the CBT worksheets is the thought record. This basic tool helps you think about your thinking. It's a series of questions that offers you a step-by-step way of identifying your negative thinking and a way to change it. This traditional worksheet starts with an event, leading to a thought and behavioral consequence, then a more rational response. Turn the page, and let's start filling out a thought log.

THOUGHT LOG

EVENT	THOUGHT	CONSEQUENCE	RATIONAL COUNTERSTATEMENT
Your friend cancels dinner plans.	"I must have done something to upset them. They probably hate me now."	Feeling anxious, lonely, and sad.	"My friend probably had something come up at the last minute. It happens to everyone. I'll reach out to them tomorrow to reschedule."

Working with Your Inner Critic Today

When you begin working with the inner critic, you are learning to recreate and rewire your thinking and your brain. It is going to feel weird and uncomfortable. Hang with it. You can create a different way, a different story for your life. The first tools to learn and practice to make the shift happen are acceptance and awareness.

Acceptance:
Your inner critic will always be there, and in the early stages of awareness it's going to become louder.

It is proven that it is possible to shift how you experience your inner critic and its impact on your life.

Awareness:
Get to know your inner critic better by answering these questions:

What does my inner critic sound like? (high pitched, low volume, soft, loud, etc.)

What does my inner critic look like? (an angry schoolmaster, a monster, a garden gnome, etc.)

What are the messages my inner critic is saying to me? (that's stupid, who do you think you are, you're ugly, what a failure, etc.).

How are these messages impacting my life?

What would I be like if I lived free of this inner critical voice?

What would it feel like?

How much less energy would I spend on worrying?

What am I learning about myself?

What one thing can I do differently as a result?

As we move into Week Three, consider these questions in order to transition yourself to the next topic: *What did I learn this week? What skills, information, or stories resonated with me? How do I feel about moving forward?*

It may be helpful for you to write down any big revelations you had about your inner critic. Since you're going to spend a lot of time getting to know it, your first impression of who that inner critic is can be a valuable go-to if you find yourself struggling to escape its voice.

CHAPTER 5
Week Three – Transforming Your Relationship with Your Thoughts

This week, we are going to work on:

* Recognizing your thought patterns;

* Identifying self-defeating thoughts; and

* Exploring fear, anxiety, and perfectionism.

We'll build on:

* What type of negative voice your inner critic uses;

* Your relationship with your inner critic; and

* Recognizing your distorted thoughts.

Feeling good and feeling self-confident are not one and the same. When we seek happiness by buying things, trying to look a different way, or through validation from another person, we are very often left feeling defeated. This is when that negative inner critic seems relentless, taking advantage of our flaws and failures in an effort to help us, but only making us spiral further into the depths of our self-doubt. Many of us will stop here, giving up and submitting to our Negative Nelly. This is the time we need self-compassion the most.

Self-compassion is the very essence of what builds self-esteem. As we peel back the layers of our inner conversations, stuff gets real! The feelings that we tend to bury deep within ourselves begin to emerge, and that scares us. This week, you will learn compelling ways to move through and cope during these challenging times of change.

Self-defeating thoughts are sometimes hard to recognize because they have become so deeply ingrained in our psyches. Our motivations, unless explored, often go unnoticed even by us, and in some cases, we are the only ones who can't see what we're doing.

Consider the case of Amelia: A woman in her 50s who had just gone shopping prior to our session. She was quite upset because her body was changing due to menopause. We talked a little bit about what parts of her body were changing and how she was talking to herself about the changes. Initially, she shared her thoughts of "feeling like an old lady." I then asked her what she needed, and she replied, "I want my old body back. I feel out of control because my body is reacting differently than it did in the past. I look like my mother!" We then discussed what she was afraid of, and clarified her feelings of fear, grief, and hopelessness. Using the compassionate techniques in this chapter, we explored her self-defeating thoughts along with her distorted thinking, and worked to separate her critical voice from her true self. We were then able to focus on accepting her changing body, and unmasking the damaging nature of her critical thoughts.

DIVING DEEPER INTO YOUR THOUGHT PATTERNS

In people with lower levels of self-confidence, we often find more negative-biased thinking, which is what leads to depression or depressive thoughts. However, we "low levelers" also tend to experience feelings of anxiety when we overestimate the likelihood that something really bad will happen and equally underestimate our ability to cope with whatever occurs.

These distortions make us feel more comfortable by offering us a way to understand our environment. Yet these narrow or grand ways of thinking take us further from the truth of our reality, needlessly applying labels which are mostly inaccurate. The result is an unbalanced and often detached view of the world—the opposite of what helps build healthy self-esteem and vulnerable connections with others.

With attention, understanding, and perseverance, you can ride the wave of these unhelpful thoughts and emerge with the confidence and resolve to keep trying!

Even counselors have days that become fraught with cognitive distortions. If we don't consistently pay attention to how we are thinking, we return to the comfort zone of automatic and reactionary thinking. Nelly returns with a vengeance! Without noticing she's back, I easily begin believing what she says and find myself feeling uncomfortable, sad, or anxious. For me, Nasty Nelly takes over when I haven't gotten enough sleep or schedule way too many clients for the week. I start to feel and behave less confidently, and my self-esteem suffers.

Catching and dissolving distorted thinking will cause you some discomfort, fear, and frustration, and you will want to quit. Your inner critic is fierce and will try to tell you it is not worth all this effort.

He/she/they will tell you it isn't working fast enough or at all—so what's the point?

The point, my friend, is you. Do you want to feel strong and secure? Do you want to be able to get your needs met? Are you willing to make a commitment to be caring and compassionate with yourself? Great—onward we go.

Each time we catch ourselves in our old patterns of distorted thinking, we give ourselves the opportunity to replace that old "stinking thinking" with a much more rational alternative. We have the opportunity to start fresh. To experience the world, our world, as it truly is. Let's take a look at two ways to do just that.

FACT OR OPINION?

As we touched on in the last chapter, facts are not opinions. Just because you think something, doesn't make it true. But even knowing that, it can be hard to tell the difference sometimes, especially when we're used to thinking negatively about ourselves or our world. Today, you will go about your life, carrying your notebook with you, and practice writing down some of the thoughts going through your head. Did you realize once you were at work that you forgot to feed the dog this morning? "I forgot to feed the dog" is a fact. But if you now think that worrying about your pet is going to derail your whole day and that everything you work on will end in disaster, that's an opinion.

STOP THE CATASTROPHE IN ITS TRACKS

Let's take some of the thoughts that bothered you most over the course of the day and work on de-catastrophizing them. Let's use the same example we used above, and say that you feel so badly about forgetting to feed your pet or are so worried about your pet that you can't focus at work. Are you now worried you're going to mess up your part in a big project? Forget a deadline? Get fired as a result? That's catastrophizing. Stopping that flood of panic may take a bit of work, but let's try. Write down what, specifically, you're worried will happen, and list anything you feel is "evidence" that this really will happen. Now, let's carry that catastrophe through to its final endpoint. If you're worried you'll get fired, then let's think that through. If you lose your job, what is the absolute worst thing that could happen as a result of that? And is that "absolute worst thing possible" actually the most likely outcome, or just the most terrible thing your mind can think of? Write down what's likelier to happen instead. Finally, take a look forward into the future. How big of a problem will this be in a month? How about in a year?

Power Posing

Back in 2012, Harvard business school professor Amy Cuddy gave her famous Ted talk on "power posing." She describes power posing as taking up a bit of space while positioning your arms and legs away from your body in an open and expansive way. Cuddy suggests that posing this way skips over psychological blocks, allowing our body to directly influence our mind.

I say hop out of bed and strike a pose.

LEARNING TO DEAL WITH YOUR THOUGHTS

As you should be able to tell from the above thought experiments, the quality of our thoughts truly matters. Between the time we wake up and the time we fall asleep, our minds are there to help us. The thoughts we allow ourselves to think are the thoughts that create our emotions. These then affect our behavior and how we relate to other people in the world. As Marcus Aurelius said, "The happiness of your life depends upon the quality of your thoughts: therefore, guard accordingly, and take care that you entertain no notions unsuitable to virtue and reasonable nature." Or as I say, "Learn to think well of yourself and therefore be well with yourself."

In learning to cope with our everyday thoughts, it's important to note that our goal should not be to eradicate them. That can't be done. I am often surprised at how many of my clients want me to teach them how to "kill" their inner critic. In learning to observe our thoughts, it's important to not categorize them as "useful" and "not useful." This is all-or-nothing thinking.

It is impossible to climb a six-foot stepladder in one step. In the case of our thought process, it is necessary to look deeper into how we think; to observe, acknowledge, examine, and accept our negative thoughts. By doing this, we don't reject a very important part of our being: the part of our mind that was meant to protect us. Instead, we lean forward and toward this part in order to learn from it. Here are some strategies to do just that.

ONALEF YOUR NEGATIVE THOUGHTS

I know what you're thinking: "*You said you didn't like acronyms, Lynn.*" You got me. But like WOOP, I find ONALEF to be a wonderful tool. Although it doesn't have as punchy of a name as WOOP, it still gets the job done. Here is how it works:

Observe without judging your emotions.

Notice the thoughts and then the feelings that emerge.

Ask yourself, "Why am I thinking like this?"

Look for evidence to support your "Why?"

Explore two to three other possibilities.

Find evidence to support one possibility.

TAKE A BREAK

If you are working overtime, or just plain working, and you can't seem to stop your mind from drifting into negative thoughts, take a break. Go outside, go for a walk, or go talk to a friend about last night's game or episode of *The Bachelor*. Feeling overwhelmed rarely works in our favor. When you get a feeling that things are not going well, it is perfectly acceptable to step away. Shifting our focus away from what we are stuck on can help us gain perspective when we come back to it.

CREATE A REAL-WORLD COMFORT ZONE

Living in the past, worrying about the future, and creating elaborate plans to make sure everything is going to be safe, happy, and healthy may be providing your subconscious with some comfort, but it is not sustainable comfort. Instead, carve out a safe place in your own environment in real life. So many of us are not taking up space in our own homes. By this, I mean your place, not your chair or your side of the bed. An actual room is fantastic, but sometimes a closet or a nook will do. It's all about putting things you love in the space you want to be in. You're creating comfort so that you want to spend time there. Here you can meditate, listen to music, and permit yourself to focus on *your* needs. It can be for five minutes or an hour or longer, just so long as it's all about you.

COST/BENEFIT ANALYSIS

A big realization for many of us is how much time and energy we spend with negative thinking. What else could we be doing? Just the time alone translates to a huge loss. The next time you catch yourself thinking "they must" or "I should," take a deep breath—a real deep breath—and ask yourself if that thought benefits you in any way. A benefit would be if it truly does protect you from harm or an emotional tsunami. If it doesn't offer a benefit, ask yourself what it is costing you to entertain that thought. Costs are things like anxiety, rumination, resentment, and other ways we punish ourselves.

Stop, Listen, and Love

This is a great technique to use and practice so that you can pull it out of your "back pocket" anytime you need it, and you can do all of it in your head. It serves as a confidence boost and a self-love boost all in one. All you have to do is jot down these questions and their answers on a note card or in your phone. You could even record a voice message to yourself to listen to when you need it. The idea is to have it be portable so that you can carry it with you most of the time.

I am at my best when . . .

This week, I have discovered that I am . . .

I gain strength from . . .

I am proud of . . .

I felt good just typing those!

ANXIETY AND FEAR

It's probably no surprise to you that anxiety has been on the rise, with a record number of people across the globe reporting a range of symptoms. But what happens when we ask people about their fears? Brené Brown has brilliantly discussed fear in many of her books, talks, and writings. On her website, she writes, "It's not fear that gets in the way of showing up—it's armor. It's the behaviors we use to self-protect. When our negative thoughts come for us, we build our wall and protect ourselves using the armor of fear and anxiety."

Frank was a client of mine who suffered greatly from anxiety. He was a hostage to it. He experienced days when he felt sick to his stomach and could barely get up to fix a meal. He was shaky most of the time. The life he wanted was one of social interactions, going to the movies, meeting people for dinner, and enjoying the companionship of a partner in life. He would often cancel plans with people because he was just too worried about what would happen. Did he have to take the metro? How long should he allow? What if he was mugged or late or got lost? He felt confined and frustrated because of his anxiety. However, what Frank truly suffered from was overwhelming fear.

Advances in neuroscience have shown us that anxiety and fear cannot be separated. Fear is an emotional response to a known threat; when faced with fear we all experience anxiety and the physical symptoms that go along with it. As we discussed earlier, this is the fight, flight, freeze, and submit stress response. One researched explanation for the increase in anxiety is our transference of stress from being harmed or eaten by ferocious sabertooths or trampled by massive mammoths to our present day attempts to process too much information on a daily basis.

If we start our days telling ourselves that we are stressed, it will likely lead to symptoms of anxiety, such as a faster heart rate, sweaty palms, sluggish thinking, and feeling jittery. This is the moment in your brain when your inner critic takes over, hijacking your finely tuned decision-making center (your prefrontal cortex) where fear and anxiety meet. Although it feels terrible, it is not how the anxiety and fear feel in your body that harms you. It may feel like you could die, but you will not. The harmful part of this vicious cycle is when you see yourself as weak, impaired, and out of control, rather than an intelligent, strong person who is in the midst of an overactive stress response.

Chronic stress and overstimulation of our stress response, which is interwoven with anxiety, fear and low self-worth/esteem/confidence, impacts our mind and body. We can experience physical symptoms, issues with our memory, interruptions in our brain's normal processes, and can even find our mental health severely impacted by the long-term effects of stress.

Learning skills to work with and confront the anxiety and fear that keep you from reaching your goals is, well, kind of scary. It's probably the reason that you bought this book. You may not have identified that you are afraid, but it is central to much of what keeps us from getting our needs met in life. Each day, we face challenges that bring about fear. How do we confront that fear and stop it from holding us back?

Over the past several years, I have let one fear hold me back from something I crave: companionship. You see, I've spent a fair amount of time online dating. After many dates that did not lead to anything of substance, I began to feel frustrated, hopeless, and lonelier than when I wasn't dating. I came to the realization that my desire to meet a good companion had evolved into anxiety and fear about the actual dating experience. It began to feel like a chore, surrounded by worry and apathy. It occurred to me that I was creating a situation of stress, inviting my stress response to engage. This, of course, was the opposite of what I needed and wanted in my life. I share this story because I know that I am not alone. And, while I have not yet fully overcome this anxiety and fear, let's take a look at a few ways I could. Of course, you could apply these things to whatever you are fearful of.

COPING AHEAD

Let's say you have severe anxiety when stuck in traffic. You can't stand it—your heart beats fast, you start to sweat when the cars slow down, and you want to run and leave the car behind. You can't get rid of all the traffic, but you can find different times to drive to work by different routes, and then use some skills to help you navigate the moment. In taking the time to plan ahead, you can familiarize yourself with some easy and efficient ways to reduce anxiety quickly:

* Accept that you cannot make your anxiety/fear fully disappear. Ask yourself to stop struggling against it and free up some much-needed energy to do something else.
* Separate yourself from the anxiety so you are not superglued to it. You are not your thoughts, your anxiety, or the last donut you ate.
* Practice mindfulness. All you need to do this is something that catches your eye and your attention: a flower on the side of the road, a beautiful color on a billboard, or the shiny building you call home.

CALL OUT VOLDEMORT

I have not yet read Harry Potter, but a friend of mine told me about this exercise. Apparently, there is an absolute fear of mentioning the true name of "He-Who-Must-Not-Be-Named." In the land of psychology, this gives Voldemort supreme power. When we hold our fears this tightly, it causes immense anxiety, and we increase the fear of sharing them with others. This gives our fears a great deal of power over us. We all have fears and dreams that we keep secret—that nobody knows but us. Maybe you can be like Harry: Name your fear, say it out loud. Even better if you do it with somebody you can trust—a friend, a counselor, or a spiritual guide.

VISUALIZE YOURSELF CALM

This tip requires you to practice the breathing techniques you've learned. After taking a few deep breaths, close your eyes and picture yourself calm. See your body relaxed and imagine yourself working through a stressful or anxiety-causing situation by staying calm and focused.

If you find yourself floating into the gray clouds of negative thoughts stemming from past fears and injustices, put both feet on the ground, both hands on your heart, and breathe. Count to 10, and then do it again.

Your Most Important Relationship

Our anxiety is a symptom of our fears. Low self-esteem raises anxiety, and anxiety decreases self-esteem. And we all come tumbling down because we berate ourselves for letting anxiety get the best of us. A good deal of anxiety stems from fear that we don't have the skills, abilities, or intelligence to be successful and loved. We learn to seek external validation to offset our fears. Just for today, let's work on practicing how to be your own best friend. Here's what you can do to get started on your relationship with yourself:

Write down the last kind thing you said about yourself. If you can't think of anything, say something now and write it down. Listen to the tone of voice you use when saying these things to yourself. Is it the same as the one you use with your friends? If it isn't, try it again using that voice.

Here is when everybody rolls their eyes at me, but I'm telling you, it works. Find your favorite color sticky note and your favorite marker. Put them next to a mirror you look in every single day. For today, write, "Am I being kind to myself?" Tomorrow, post a different question to yourself in words of friendship and compassion.

I'VE CONFRONTED MY THOUGHTS, BUT WHAT ABOUT EVERYONE ELSE'S?

There's no getting around it, criticism sucks. It makes us question ourselves and hurts like hell. But the very worst thing is that it often makes us give up. Sure, if we have healthy self-esteem, we may opt to separate ourselves from the feedback without it shaking our perception of ourselves. However, as people with lower self-esteem and confidence, we usually react in one of two ways.

If you base your confidence on external sources of validation, you are much more likely to either overreact or underreact to any type of negative or constructive feedback. In other words, we may distort our thinking around the feedback. We may catastrophize, apply black-and-white thinking, or even "mindread" in between and all around what was said.

I am going to go out on a limb here and say 99 percent of us really don't like getting feedback, constructive or otherwise, and oftentimes we can make both ourselves and the giver of the feedback uncomfortable with our reaction.

Here are a few options for listening to, responding to, coping with, and accepting the feedback of other people:

Explore your feelings: One of the first distorted thinking problems that emerges is jumping to conclusions—you'll do it before you even get in the room with the person. Allowing yourself to explore these feelings prior to the feedback session is highly encouraged. If you can take a step back from the very first reaction that is brewing inside of you, you might identify what you fear most about the upcoming interaction. Working through some of the other exercises we've gone over previously might help.

Be aware of yourself: Take notice of your body language. While this is a bigger discussion, it's good to know if you are an eyeroller, an armcrosser, or a frowner. These are best avoided as they can greatly distract both you and the person you're sitting across from, causing a lack of healthy communication between both of you.

Pay attention: Listen well to understand what is being said. What is the first thing that comes to mind when someone criticizes you? If your mind is racing with thoughts like, "But that's not what I meant!" or, "I was only doing what you told me to"; or if you're already preparing a list of reasons why the way you did things was, in fact, the right way, then you are likely not listening closely because you're internally defending yourself.

This is such a great way to end this chapter, because it's something we've all run into. It shines a real-life light on how we tend to see ourselves through the eyes of others. When we are required to sit formally with someone—professionally or personally—for the sole purpose of being given feedback, it can be messy internally for those seeking better confidence and self-esteem.

As we move into Week Four, consider these questions in order to transition yourself to the next topic: *What did I learn this week? What skills, tips, or stories resonated with me? How do I feel about moving forward?*

Consider writing down a list of bullet points of anything you realized about your own thought patterns. If you're defensive, or if you're having trouble imagining being kind to yourself, laying out that discovery now can give you a helpful point of reference next time you find yourself engaging in old thought patterns.

CHAPTER 6
Week Four - Beliefs and Values

This week, we are going to:

* Discover where your beliefs and values come from;

* Discover how they affect your self-confidence and esteem; and

* Discover how to decide to keep them or let them go.

We'll build on:

* The goals you have set;

* Your strengths, motivation, and readiness;

* Your self-improvement priorities; and

* What you have learned about your thinking.

So much of how we think and behave builds and broadens over our lifetime. The beauty and purpose of self-exploration is magnified by determining what you want to achieve, knowing which strengths will move you forward, building awareness of how you speak to yourself, and making sure you are able to recognize the positive impact self-compassion and transforming your thoughts have on your self-confidence and self-esteem.

You and I are constantly making choices, moving backwards or forwards, writing or rewriting our stories. All of these actions matter and offer us the opportunity to explore what lies beneath them. By reflecting on your internal voice, you will increase your awareness of your intentions, dreams, beliefs, and values. I am encouraging you to notice the hidden stories, the discussions happening between you and your inner critic subconsciously, behind your day-to-day actions. For many, noticing an action that we don't like creates discomfort, so it often gets overlooked, rejected, or numbed. Our inner critic will fight back if we allow it to. It will continue its warring ways inside our souls and bodies using our beliefs and values as weapons against us.

This week, we will take an even closer look at the origins of your inner critic. How does it know which "should, would, and coulds" make us feel the worst? Where does the seemingly endless supply of these self-defeating comments come from? This, dear ones, is how we locate your pivot point, where you cross the threshold and shift your momentum, notice the light, and tune into your ability to experience massive change!

Let's begin our journey into discovering where all these negative thoughts come from by looking at a great quote: "Comparison is the thief of joy." Sometimes it's attributed to Theodore Roosevelt and other times to Mark Twain, but whomever said it, it regularly appears on my social media feeds. It is such a relevant connection for the age of selfies, when we're living our lives constantly assessing whether or not what we are doing is "Instagrammable." I recently witnessed a heartbreaking conversation on social media started by someone

I truly admire for her perseverance and accomplishments in the online realm of addiction recovery. She posted about her concerns regarding her "relevance," expressing, with great vulnerability, how she felt her age, looks, and lack of ability to grow her following to more than her current 3,000+ people meant that she was not worthy of continuing her work. Nearly 150 followers chimed in with support, mainly in the form of voicing similar types of self-doubt and insecurities. Can you relate? What was so very heartbreaking was the many toxic core beliefs I read in her and her many followers' posts.

One of the most common core belief and value issues that clients come to me with is conflict in the workplace. Eddie came to me wanting to address his high stress level and frustration with his job. His company had just been purchased by a much larger company, and many changes were in motion. He had held his C-level position for 12 years and had long established his system for doing things, and now that was all about to change. Since he was in his mid-40s and had not completed his undergraduate degree, he felt he was truly lucky to have risen to such a high level. The first big changes came when the company introduced new technology, including video conferencing, and new workflow, accounting, and internal communication software. He felt like they were making a mistake by trying all these new things that seemed unnecessary and difficult to learn. Eddie also began to complain about how other people were showing off and bragging about how fast they could learn the new systems, mostly because they were young and educated. When I asked him what he was most afraid of, he responded with some telling information about his core beliefs and values. He used phrases like "I look dumb," "I can't pick these things up so quickly," "I hate these changes," and "I should be able to learn this stuff faster." In this session, Eddie took his first steps toward uncovering some of his most self-destructive core beliefs.

WHAT ARE BELIEFS AND VALUES?

Just like distinguishing self-esteem from self-confidence, identifying the difference between core beliefs and core values can be a bit confusing. They both guide our actions and behaviors, but they differ greatly in how they motivate us. Take a look at the iceberg pictured on the next page. What is above the waterline is what we can see—our behaviors and abilities. This is our conscious self. Below the waterline is our unconscious self, an inverted pyramid with our beliefs closest to the waterline, followed by our values and our self-concept (self-esteem and confidence) at the peak. I call this our "Selfberg," an adaption from one of the pioneers in family therapy, Virginia Satir, and her metaphor of an iceberg representing our inner world.

Looking at the Selfberg diagram, you might notice that only about 10 percent of yourself is above the waterline. That's what you are conscious of. These are the components that mostly work to improve our self-confidence; it's our comfort zone of *what* we can do and *how* we can do it. Most of us rely on this "tip of the iceberg" to determine our sense of self, or who we think we are. But what about the other 90 percent? What lies beneath in our subconscious mind?

This is where being curious about your relationship with yourself gets truly interesting. If we only pay attention to our external behaviors and abilities, those things that we present with confidence to others, how do we build a true and trusting relationship with ourselves? This is the question that will lead to overall improved self-esteem. I'll never forget the feeling I got when I first came across the quote by Denis Waitley, "It's not what you are that holds you back, it's what you think you are not." It stunned me. What? Aren't they one and the same? They are not. Mind sufficiently blown.

CONSCIOUS

EXTERNAL SELF

ABILITIES

BEHAVIOR

BELIEFS

VALUES

SUBCONSCIOUS

Since many of us confuse beliefs and values, let's first make clear the differences between them. Our beliefs are assumptions and convictions we develop over time and use as a steering wheel of sorts. They don't require any proof or facts to support them and often grow from within, using our experiences and internal, subconscious monologue. Our inner critic is the amplifier of our **negative** beliefs.

Our values originate from our beliefs about the people, places, and things we hold in high regard. The core of our values is rooted in a particular belief most often related to worth—of a behavior, idea, or life decision determined by various cultural norms. Our values guide us to judge what is right or wrong. As with beliefs, values are usually not based on empirical evidence or even rational thought. However, where beliefs can be adjusted or changed with persuasion, time, or evidence, values are pretty stubborn and resistant to change. Our values are the ever-running engine for our self-confidence and self-esteem.

Evidence of your current state of self-worth (your mix of confidence and esteem) can be uncovered by examining your insecurities and critical thoughts. I know, not fun, but all the reading and work you have done so far has been in preparation for this! All of us who have struggled with low self-worth and crippling insecurities know firsthand that we cannot simply talk ourselves out of that dim hole. In order to reprogram and reset our subconscious mind toward more confidence and better self-esteem, we need to address our beliefs and the values that support them. Take a look at the following lists and see if you can find your beliefs and values.

Beliefs are often declarative statements. I believe:

* I don't deserve this.
* I am never good enough.
* I can never get/do what I want.
* I deserve to be happy.
* I need to be successful.
* Lying is okay in some circumstances.
* Lying is never okay.

Values are typically more conceptual and easily verbalized. I value:

* Honesty
* Integrity
* Family
* Religion
* Peace
* Curiosity
* Education
* Equality
* Perseverance

Lost in Translation

When we look at a list of values, even the short one I shared, we often have great difficulty narrowing the list down to the most important ones, and identifying how those values affect us daily. Just for today, choose one of the nine listed. Really, only one. Now, take a look at your habits, hour by hour. These daily habits are how we live our values. Can you find the moments you are truly living your values? How long have these habits been a part of your daily life?

WHERE DO BELIEFS AND VALUES COME FROM?

Up to this point, we have worked to uncover unhealthy thoughts and feelings that may interfere with your goals of achieving healthy and good self-confidence and self-esteem. In an effort to build even more self-awareness, we need to do a little bit of time travel. You may not want to and I get it. Many people come to my office explicitly saying, "I do not want to discuss my childhood," but even if I don't ask, they always, *always* end up sharing stories of their time growing up. We cannot help it; the desire to connect is hardwired into us.

BELIEFS

As children, we develop at least three core beliefs that continue to affect us today. It's impossible to understand ourselves in the present moment without examining at least some of our past. These beliefs, born out of our interactions, our experiences, and what we learn from our caretakers, can be positive or negative.

Beliefs about yourself: Our childhoods give us a pretty clear sense of who we are as a person through the eyes of our parents, siblings, aunts, uncles, cousins, peers, and teachers. They give us the basis of knowledge about our personality traits, our abilities, and, of course, our values. We develop a narrative: stories about how we look, how we perform in school, and our skills in activities such as art, music, or sports.

Beliefs about others: We are taught pretty early on to observe and learn about other people. Most of us learned that our success in life comes from the approval of others. How someone appears to be from the outside begins to be prioritized over our true selves. We learn the unfortunate art of comparison.

Beliefs about the world: There are core beliefs we learn about the world. First, is it safe or unsafe? This shapes whether we see the world optimistically or pessimistically. If you experience a chaotic, harsh, or even traumatic environment, the world will likely seem like a scary place to you. You learn to see the world as a place in which you must struggle in order to succeed.

VALUES

Values also develop in our early years, formed by specific beliefs that relate to the worth of an idea, behavior, or person. Values are mostly learned and adopted from our families of origin and the culture in which we are raised, and influenced by peers, media, religion, education, and technology. Sociologist Morris Massey describes the three periods in which values develop as we grow as the Imprint Period (when we absorb everything we can from everyone around us), the Modeling Period (when we copy what we see and maybe try out a few different ways of existing in the world), and the Socialization Period (when we find others like us and look to our peers for guidance).

Just as so many of us fully trust and believe in the accuracy of our inner critical voice, we also tend to accept that our beliefs and values are set in stone. We allow them to operate mostly in our subconscious, and they comfort us because they often become automatic behaviors. They run our day-to-day lives silently and powerfully. The beliefs about the work we do, our religious and spiritual ideas, our loyalty to family, and other beliefs and values passed down from generation to generation may guide us in helpful ways, but they can also take too much control and trap us in violent or chaotic behaviors. Controlling beliefs and values are often apparent when people invoke a tribalistic "us versus them" way of life.

How this plays out in our day-to-day lives is a combination of three self-defeating mechanisms: distorted thinking, lack of self-awareness, and confirmation bias. If our behavior is controlled by a belief and/or value we have adopted without investigation or challenge, we will endlessly seek to confirm it so as to protect our self-concept and self-esteem. One way this becomes evident in our daily life is in feeling insecure or invalidated about your opinions. You may also often feel overly criticized by others and perhaps defensive about your ideas, decisions, or skills. Confirmation bias is the tendency to process information, relationships, politics, and more by looking for, or *interpreting*, information that only supports and is consistent with our existing beliefs, values, and opinions. When we are confronted with the possibility that what we have long believed or highly valued may not be accurate or may have caused us inner discord, our inner critic will usually try to step in and take us down the rumination hole of self-loathing.

A delightful truth is that we are meant to be in control of our beliefs and values, not the other way around! By uncovering and understanding what is important to you and why, you will be able to be more confident in the decisions you make. Getting clear on what you believe and value helps your self-esteem get laser sharp about who you are and what you stand for. You can decide which values and beliefs are sabotaging your self-worth. When you are certain about your beliefs and values, you will seek out and spend your energy on those people, organizations, and movements that align with you, leaving behind those that do not.

This process of discovering, clarifying, focusing, and shedding has allowed me and those I help to accept beneficial values and beliefs, and reject those that no longer serve us. This is deconstructing. Reconstructing is what brings about sustainable and lasting transformation in our development-of-self department! It is how we go from frustration to fulfillment. It's how we move from believing we are not deserving of love, success, and happiness to a more harmonious reality built on active awareness and insight of who we are and what we believe in.

Which Beliefs and Values Do You Focus On?

Which list better represents how you would describe yourself and the way you live today?

List #1

* Accountable
* Balanced
* Challenged
* Compassionate
* Confident
* Dependable
* Ethical
* Free
* Happy
* Secure
* Joyful
* Wise

List #2

* Anxious
* Angry
* Critical
* Frustrated
* Guilty
* Lonely
* Regretful
* Sad
* Self-doubting
* Withdrawn
* Worried

If you align more with the first list, you tend to focus on positive values and beliefs.

And—you guessed it—if you align more with the second list, you focus more on negative values and beliefs.

EFFECTS OF BELIEFS AND VALUES

Was choosing a list difficult for you? I'm going to guess you really wanted to choose list #1 even if you experience more of the things on #2. If you decided to skip choosing altogether, you are not alone! This quiz is meant to stimulate your inner critic and get it on the defensive. I want you to hear what that nasty little voice is saying to you. It is an insidious force. You are reading this book, moving toward self-improvement, and your Nasty Nelly comes from the deep and tries to sabotage your progress. Our inner critics attempt to lure and lull us with "comforting" self-protective thoughts, thoughts that sound friendly, like "Shouldn't you be spending time doing something more important?" or "This isn't what you need," confusing us and derailing us from our goals.

CONSCIOUS

EXTERNAL SELF

ABILITIES   BEHAVIOR

BELIEFS

VALUES

TRUE SELF

SUBCONSCIOUS

Looking again at the Selfberg, identify one of your goals from Week One, and let's walk through the diagram. As an example, say one of your goals was to improve your awareness of "who you really are," your true self—a pretty common desire. In Week Two, you began to familiarize yourself with how your inner critic was speaking to you and how to begin the process of interrupting it. In Week Three, your focus became how to identify your patterns of thought and how they triggered anxiety, fear, and behaviors, and ways to confront your own Nasty Nellie. Now, we unpack the layering effect of beliefs over values on top of self-concept governing and steering our daily lives.

We start at the top with core beliefs; these are our convictions that we hold to be true regardless of any evidence. The most powerful of our beliefs is mostly negative and toxic to our self-esteem. There are two core beliefs that most influence our overall sense of self-worth, affecting our self-image and well-being: the belief of what success is and the belief in our own lovability. These beliefs encourage us to behave in ways that support and confirm the following inner biases: "I'm a failure, I'm not good enough, and I can never do anything right" and "I don't fit in. I will be rejected and people always leave me."

These harmful core beliefs are developed in direct response to our core values, needs, and desires, and are geared toward the feelings of safety, belonging, and being loved. Our natural notion is to move toward what feels good and avoid what does not. It is when these values and beliefs morph into righteous internal demands and rules—the "should"—that we begin to have difficulties with our self-esteem and confidence. This is what Karen Horney, a German psychoanalyst who practiced in the United States, referred to as the "tyranny of the should." She also called this the "hopeless search for glory"—the ever-present feeling that somehow we are not living up to our ideal selves. We torture ourselves with all kinds of expectations that we would never place on our loved ones. We become paralyzed when faced with meeting the expectations of ourselves and others, instead of living according to our deepest desires. I see this as living *incongruently* with our most authentic self.

HEALTHY VALUES VERSUS UNHEALTHY VALUES

You are worthy! The tension and restlessness you may feel at this point is your intuition attempting to break through. Your inner compass will be feeling a bit wonky during this period of exploration. I believe that so much of the anxiety and depression felt in this world is due to living our lives in accordance with values and beliefs we truly don't accept. As we become more aware of what we value most, we get curious about whether our beliefs and values are mostly healthy or unhealthy. It can be massively overwhelming for us to apply the many subjective theories of measuring healthy versus unhealthy. To illustrate this, I will use examples of beliefs about our lovability and success. If you have the belief that you are unlovable, you are likely being guided by a high regard for the core values of needing to be loved and to belong.

EXAMPLE ONE: GEORGE

George is a 43-year-old who recently quit his government job to pursue his dream of woodworking, creating unique furnishings, and working from home. His father is a well-known former diplomat who has always been disappointed that George didn't express more interest in becoming a diplomat himself. George has not shared his plan with his father and feels heavy with guilt and a sense that he is letting his father down, once again. His wife was surprised that on his first full day working at home he was not in his shop, and he confided in her that he felt "his whole life has been irrelevant."

What is going on below George's surface? George is being rigid based on his father's idea of what a relevant and successful life is. He has long been tortured by his father's rules and values, which he has blindly accepted. He is also denying that he truly enjoys woodworking and ignores his own desires, comparing himself to his father and his desires.

EXAMPLE TWO: TORY

Tory knows two things for sure: that she is attracted to women and that her mother doesn't love her. She is currently married to Tom and has been extremely unhappy for most of their six years together. After confessing that she is a lesbian, she and Tom have agreed to divorce, but continue to live together and "pretend" to be a couple. Her mother always told her that her marriage to Tom should come first, and that it is a woman's job to be a "good wife" no matter what she needs to sacrifice. Tory is terrified of her mother's response and has decided not to tell her, hoping she can live her life without her mother's interference.

What's going on under the surface with Tory? Tory is attempting to be flexible with her own life while rigidly controlling the information she gives her mother. While she has examined her own desires and needs, she continues to live by her mother's value of self-sacrifice by hiding her emotional pain and pretending to still be married to Tom.

HOW TO THINK ABOUT BELIEFS AND VALUES IN A HEALTHY WAY

Our beliefs are those ideas we hold to be true even if irrational or unproven. We have developed them from what we have seen, heard, read, and experienced over time; they steer us in certain directions. In order to make more sense of these "inner rules," we prioritized a set of values (based on these beliefs/rules), letting those which we hold out as most important guide our decisions. Our behaviors are how we act on these beliefs and values, so then why do we sometimes act/behave out of alignment with our values, which then causes discomfort, discontent, and dilemmas in our lives?

The Selfberg diagram shows the relationship between our subconscious belief and values system and our conscious behaviors and abilities. But what is it, then, that influences our behaviors that sometimes throws us off course? Let me introduce you to your most sassy and salty inner voice: attitude.

Our attitudes are the immediate feeling, thought, or knee-jerk reaction or response to someone or something. Researchers and theorists toss around a lot of fancy language to describe attitudes. In a professional setting we might say that attitudes are hypothetical constructs that represent a person's likes or dislikes. But let's get real: Attitudes are our personal judgments about others and our circumstances. We access our attitudes before we make decisions about how to behave. Carl Jung, the prominent Swiss psychiatrist and psychoanalyst, defined attitudes as "the readiness of the psyche to act or react in a certain way."

We develop our attitudes by applying a filter over the behavior of other people and ourselves. The filter arises from our internal core beliefs and values and is cheered on by our thoughts. We may be aware of our attitudes sometimes, but we aren't at other times. They're also not always working in sync with our actual behavior. And when that happens—when our attitudes along with our beliefs and values aren't matching up with how we're presenting ourselves to the world—our self-esteem and self-confidence suffer greatly.

SELF-CONTROL VERSUS SELF-REGULATION

Most of us think about self-control in terms of our willfulness and restraint, our ability to control all those emotions bubbling beneath our surface by silencing them. In fact, it is just the opposite. What we are in need of is much more attainable and based in our acceptance of our own cognitive abilities and competencies. This is called self-regulation or emotional regulation. We create an illusion of self-control by overestimating our abilities to influence and direct a specific or desired outcome. Control is by far the most dominant self-belief, dictating whether we pursue our goals in life to satisfy ourselves or others. Remember internal versus external motivation from Week One? If you are more externally focused, you likely feel mostly out of control of your destiny, often blaming luck, fate, or circumstances. In this mind-set, you will often choose to avoid things. Conversely, if you have a strong belief that you can control your perceptions, you will strive for personal development, taking accountability for your own failures and successes. Sounds reasonable, right? Enter perfectionism.

THE PRISON OF PERFECTIONISM

Perfectionism is a prison because of its ability to capture us in the ultimate self-defeating loop. Perfectionism is one of the most rigid and destructive human personality types and it has seeped into every aspect of our collective world consciousness.

Perfectionism is born from a need to stay safe in our young worlds. Safety is not only about avoiding broken bones or flesh wounds; it can be as simple as being rewarded for not causing any trouble. Children who grow up in chaotic homes where substance abuse and mental health issues are part of the family culture often develop some form of perfectionism. While perfectionism can be helpful in some situations, it mostly leads to anxiety, depression, substance abuse, and other mental health issues. Many of us (I'm a recovering perfectionist) suffer from very low self-esteem developed from our fear of disapproval from others and strong feelings of inadequacy. Over time, our inner critic gets louder as we focus on being perfect. We learn to justify our behavior as "healthy, useful, and productive" because we "get stuff done." In the long run, however, this attitude only leads to lower self-confidence and esteem, stemming from the fact that you can never live up to the preposterous expectations you set for yourself.

Am I a Perfectionist?

For this quiz, ask yourself these six yes or no questions. If you answer yes to more than three, there may be a seat in the Perfectionism Arena for you.

1. Have you spent 20 to 30 minutes writing and rewriting a brief email?

2. Have you had difficulty being happy when others experience success?

3. Did someone let you down today because they didn't do what you expected them to?

4. Do you focus on an outcome and miss learning something new?

5. Have you avoided something because it couldn't be done to your standards?

6. Have you avoided trying something new because you knew you weren't yet good at it?

FLEXIBILITY

The key to striving for excellence is flexibility. Our rigid rules/beliefs steer us toward valuing being over-competent and useful in order to feel as if we are worthy. Our self-esteem then becomes reliant on this fixed, rigid, unattainable belief. What if it were possible to set aside the ridiculous ideal of behaving perfectly? What if you could move past the ideal dinner party, hitting or surpassing your work goals, or getting all A's or five-star reviews? We're smart; we know that being and doing things perfectly is impossible! So why do we keep trying? Just like substances, sex, and gambling, perfectionism keeps us from feeling uncomfortable. It is yet another example of how we prioritize our feelings about our own behaviors. In this case, we don't desire *being* perfect, we desire *feeling* perfect. We have a negative attitude toward imperfection because it may mean we won't be loved. In our minds, perfection equals acceptance, and imperfection equals rejection.

This all-or-nothing distorted and polarized mind-set keeps us stuck believing our basic abilities and purpose are fixed traits. We only get so much, and that is it. We must take advantage of what we have and use it to our full potential in case we lose it. We hold tight to our ways because we are afraid that we are not enough. But that is not true. We are not finite—we are abundant and creative humans with the ability to learn, change, and grow.

How Flexible Are You?

Do you accept a certain ideal of who you should be? Our core beliefs set our "rules for living" and become our primary strategies for coping. Take this quiz to find out if you have rigid or flexible rules for yourself. Simply answer yes or no and be sure to check your self-honesty.

* You have difficulty making decisions.
* You rarely let anyone see "all of you."
* You like to make others happy by giving them what they want.
* You must be very good at whatever you do in front of others.
* You don't share your feelings often.
* You rarely ask for anything from another person.
* You avoid conflict at home.
* You avoid conflict at work.
* You like a good list, and have a daily routine that needs little adjustment.
* You would rather not try something with others unless you have researched it and/or practiced it.

Mostly Yes = Rigid

Mostly No = Flexible

CREATING NEW BELIEFS

Have you ever had a friend that buys every single self-improvement or "habits of success" book that comes out? Well, I was that friend. Fast-forward 10 years, and now I see a lot of this with my coaching and counseling clients. Some of them will come in with a litany of books that they've read and loved, but they just can't seem to make any progress with their issue or problem. They talk about some of the authors as if they are godlike, and sometimes even quote from the book about what so-and-so recommended they should do. One such client came to my office wanting to explore ways to become more financially independent and successful in their business. They were plagued by thoughts of self-doubt around how quickly they could become "the best" or around becoming a real "badass" in their field, while at the same time wanting to be "authentic" and "live [my] dreams." I want to be very transparent here and tell you that I get giddy when clients tell me this. It means they are on the precipice, the edge of a new way of thinking and being.

When we've accepted our confusion and our current state, we can finally start to examine the lives we're living. We start to recognize that not all of our thoughts are true, and in doing so, we start to wonder if that means our beliefs and values aren't necessarily true either.

By examining your personal values, you discover what's truly important to you. A gentle way of doing this is taking a look back on your life—to identify when you felt really good, supported by role models and mentors, and really confident that you were making good choices.

As we move into Week Five, consider these questions in order to transition yourself to the next topic: *What did I learn this week? What skills, information, or stories resonated with me? How do I feel about moving forward?*

You may find it helpful to write down any beliefs or values you do not think are true for you right now, even if they once were. As you go through your day, imagine what kinds of things you might do and say differently if you decided you no longer wanted to live your life in accordance with them.

CHAPTER 7
Week Five – Communication

This week, we are going to:

✱ Discover how communication works to build self-confidence and esteem;

✱ Learn how to care for yourself by communicating assertively; and

✱ Find out how to create self-esteem by building boundaries.

We'll build on:

✱ Your knowledge of healthy and unhealthy values and beliefs;

✱ Your understanding of your attitude's effect on your behaviors; and

✱ Your chosen and accepted old and new beliefs.

This. Is. My. Favorite. Thing. To. Talk. About.

Remember way back in the intro, I told you that you would discover the one area that, when attended to properly, would drastically improve your self-esteem and confidence? Well, here it is: communication. One of the major negative consequences of lower self-esteem and self-confidence is a marked inability to communicate our needs, desires, and feelings with nearly everyone in our lives. Communication is woven through the very fabric of our beings, and it is changing fast for us humans. Our technology is creating both bridges and roadblocks in how we communicate, and it is affecting the evolution of our species.

One of my clients, Lisa, came to me in an attempt to overcome her social awkwardness and fear of talking to other people. She thought communicating with people in social media groups might be a lifeline for her, offering a means to form healthy connections and friendships without the anxiety of an in-person interaction. Many of us confuse shyness with introversion, which is characterized by being introspective and quiet, with focus on internal thoughts. For introverts, time spent alone recharges them for more social contact. But Lisa wasn't introverted—she was acutely shy, meaning she desperately wanted to connect with others but was filled with fear and apprehension at the thought of talking to someone.

We began working on building her confidence around simple one-to-one communication by mapping out a four-step plan to meet with a friend.

1. Arrange to meet in a quiet, comfortable, and known location, like your favorite coffee shop, ice cream spot, or park.

2. Practice showing interest and asking open-ended questions, such as, "Tell me more about your trip to Italy."

3. Ask for a moment to think your answer through. Pausing usually creates some curiosity for what you might say!

4. Tell your friend/acquaintance when you need to go. Prepare the other person for a conclusion for an easier and more graceful exit.

Over the course of a month, Lisa was able to implement these steps. She felt more confident and less fearful and anxious, which enabled her to take more steps toward improving her overall confidence in social situations.

WHAT IS COMMUNICATION?

To communicate, we engage in an exchange of information, ideas, thoughts, and emotions. This can be done verbally through speaking and writing, and nonverbally through appearance, body language, and our tone of voice, volume, or rate of speech. Simple, yes?

But to communicate *effectively* with others, we must create some kind of connection. This connection allows for a flow of feelings, ideas, and thoughts, which ideally leads to a mutual understanding. I make it sound easy; I know! So many of us take the whole process of interpersonal communication for granted, making assumptions largely based on distorted thoughts such as, "They should know that about me" (blaming and should-ing) or any statement that begins with, "I think they think ... " (mind reading/jumping to conclusions).

WHAT IS INTERPERSONAL COMMUNICATION?

Interpersonal communication skills offer us ways to show understanding and respect, resolve conflicts, express our positive and negative feelings, assert our needs and boundaries, and listen to others do the same. We learn these very important skills through our caretakers, family, peers, and teachers. The benefits of learning and practicing healthy interpersonal communication skills are many: stress reduction, resolution of differences, enhanced intimacy, improved connection to others, and an increase in happy interactions.

The Big Pause

Self-awareness is a significant part of improving your relationship with yourself and others. You can become conscious of what you are thinking and feeling, and why, by practicing focusing your attention inward. Before you can listen or respond to others, you need to first listen and be compassionate with yourself. Just for today, be more attentive to the subconscious messages you are conveying to yourself. What are your feelings about the situation? When you feel the urge to respond *too quickly* to someone, take The Big Pause, and ask, "Do I subconsciously pass these same messages and feelings onto others?"

WHAT DOES COMMUNICATION HAVE TO DO WITH SELF-CONFIDENCE?

Our need for connection and belonging is strong. With every positive social interaction, we increase feelings of well-being and build hope for more of these positive emotions and interactions. When we don't have our attitudes, feelings, and desires validated in our younger years, it directly affects how we learn to feel about and communicate with ourselves. We learn how to communicate through these early intimate relationships. If our families lacked healthy communication skills, and we did not learn and practice these skills elsewhere, it is very likely our self-confidence and esteem have been negatively impacted.

The way we communicate reveals how we feel about ourselves (our self-esteem). If you are able to speak honestly, assertively, and clearly, and to listen with compassion, you've got skills! These skills are the ability to know your needs, desires, and feelings, and to verbalize them while setting boundaries. The more intense and intimate your relationship is, the more difficult the practice of these skills becomes. This, in turn, releases our unhealthier ways of coping, like our inner critic and distorted thinking.

This is why many of us find ourselves in chronic loops of unhealthy and unsatisfying intimate relationships. Self-esteem and how we communicate affect how much love and affection we are able to give and receive. Our personal history and level of self-esteem is a good predictor of relationship satisfaction. And our level of relationship satisfaction relies greatly on our ability to communicate our needs and boundaries. If you, as Lisa did, believe others should know what you are thinking instead of clearly telling them what you are thinking, feeling, and why, you may want to focus more of your attention within. Find out what you are feeling and why you feel it. Is the way you are currently communicating working for you? Let's take a closer look.

HOW DO YOU COMMUNICATE?

We can benefit greatly by noticing how we communicate with others in our daily lives. Over time, we tend to create patterns of communication which may be ineffective. Take a few moments to reflect on how you communicate with the most important people in your life by answering a few questions. Try to think and visualize your conversations with your most open and honest "eyes" as possible.

* Do I show interest by giving people my undivided attention?
* Do I try to anticipate what other people are going to say or how they might react to my words?
* Do I consider my way of doing things to be the best or most effective?
* Do I have unconscious or conscious expectations of what I want from my conversations with others?
* Do I verbalize what I need from others?
* Do I ask other people questions to gain more clarity about their feelings?
* Do I ask others about their opinions? Why and when do I ask others for their opinions?

YOU CAN'T ALWAYS GET WHAT YOU WANT

Clickbait lists of tips for better communication are one of my least favorite things in the whole wide world of the interweb. These lists often promise improvement in your relationship in "Three Easy Steps." Ugh. I have found that these quick fix promises are unhelpful and possibly damaging. This is because we don't communicate only with our words, but also with our state of emotional wellness. If you think your partner is being rude or insensitive, neuroscientists can see your "inner truths," the judgments you make based on nonverbal language long before your brain processes the actual words spoken in explanation. Trying to sugarcoat your reaction with lovely and kind language will only make you appear disingenuous. Your feelings and emotional needs will not be changed by pretty or soft language.

NEEDS VERSUS WANTS

Nearly 80 years ago, Abraham Maslow gave us his famous Hierarchy of Needs and "A Theory of Human Motivation." Before his death in 1970, he extended his idea to include our intrinsic curiosity, and gave us a framework for identifying how humans move through stages which meet our needs—from the physical needs of food, water, warmth, and rest, to security and safety, then on to belonging and love.

If you've never heard of Maslow's Hierarchy of Needs, here's what you need to know: Maslow theorized we couldn't attain self-realization—couldn't be the true selves we were supposed to be—without first having some other necessities in place. His hierarchy is depicted as a pyramid. At the bottom, representing the basic necessities we absolutely must have to survive, are things like food, water, sleep, and shelter. After we've achieved that, we move one step up on the pyramid to our safety needs—we need to be free of fear in order to thrive, so we look to protect ourselves with things like law and order. Then, we can move another step up, finding love. "Love" here encompasses everyone from our friends and families all the way to our colleagues at work. We need that social environment to succeed! After that, nearing the very top of the pyramid, is what you've been reading about all along here: our self-esteem. We need to respect ourselves and to feel respect from others. Then, and only then, can we reach the top of the pyramid and attain self-realization.

TUNING INTO WHAT YOU NEED

Thoughts uncover feelings which reveal our needs. When we encounter difficult situations, we believe our thoughts and behave accordingly. Imagine a series of lights in our mind, brain, and body—much akin to a traffic light. These are our feelings attempting to warn us to stop, go, and slow down. When we ignore our feelings, we also lose out on important information. This is how far too many of us live, without giving proper attention to our feelings. We speed along the winding roads of life, relying on our thoughts alone. As you approach a curve along your life road trip, your stomach may tighten and your heart rate increases, but you think, "I've got this!" And you charge along into the unknown. You may think you are in control, but are you?

In order for this thought to "win," you must stifle your feelings about taking the curve. We do this by judging our feelings, usually calling them "bad" or "useless." The curve could represent feeling angry at someone who mistreats you, but not being able to tell them or anyone else because you don't want to cause a problem. Your intention is to feel less stress, but the problem lingers, unresolved, and you end up feeling worse.

When was the last time you asked yourself, "What is it I need right now?" What is the feeling you are longing for? For most of us, the feeling we crave is nestled somewhere between connection and belonging. If you need acceptance, you may instead judge your partner. If you need intimacy, you may leap to trying to impress and entertain them rather than show any vulnerability. You may crave peace and harmony but avoid the problem to sidestep any kind of conflict. This is the work of becoming more knowledgeable about ourselves in order to get our needs met by being accountable to ourselves. It's difficult to satisfy a craving if we can't name it.

The most effective way of sharing feelings begins with two elusive words: "I feel ... " How much time have you spent trying to fill in the blank after those words? For me, the answer would be the first 46 years of my life. But instead, many of us may use the phrase "You make me feel," which leads us into a hollow and circular discussion of who felt what first.

It's important to learn to separate your thoughts, feelings, and needs. Using thoughts as detours from feelings or trying to think our way out of our feelings usually leads to more harmful thoughts of resentment and rumination. It distracts us from finding solutions to the deeper issue or meeting the needs that lie beneath our feelings.

THOUGHTS VERSUS FEELINGS

The majority of us label our thoughts as feelings, mostly out of habit. We weren't taught to listen for the difference or allowed to feel and express certain things. A common thought and statement is, "I feel stupid." This is a thought pretending to be a feeling. What most of us feel when we think we are stupid is shame, embarrassment, or hurt. Learning to be more accurate with describing our feelings is important to expressing our needs, getting them met, and building our confidence and self-esteem.

Since our thoughts are what we use to mask our feelings, let's use this exercise to unmask the many possible feelings that are underneath one thought.

If you think, *"I am unloved,"* you may feel:

* Vulnerable
* Abandoned
* Empty
* Worthless
* Discouraged
* Insecure
* Lonely
* Rejected
* Unimportant

If you do not acknowledge one or more of these feelings, you will continue to be distracted with thoughts such as:

* *I can't.*
* *I don't care anymore.*
* *I don't count.*
* *I don't know how.*
* *I don't matter.*
* *I give up.*
* *I'm useless.*
* *I'm worthless.*
* *I'm not good enough for you.*
* *Nobody loves me.*
* *Nobody cares.*
* *I'm not needed anymore.*
* *Nobody wants me.*
* *I'll never love again.*
* *What's wrong with me?*

How Are Your Feelings?

Most of us get asked how we feel about something every day. The next time someone asks you this question, think about your answer. Is it actually a feeling? If you're saying, "I feel sad about that" or "That makes me feel scared," then yes! But most of us automatically answer with a thought instead. You may even notice that your answer to "How do you feel about … " begins with "I think … "

CARING FOR YOURSELF WITH HEALTHY COMMUNICATION

It often surprises my clients to learn how many of our sessions will circle back to communication. There is great irony in the fact that many of my clients are high-functioning, successful individuals who initially come to see me to reduce stress and anxiety only to learn that their deeper issues are from inattention to their own needs. Most of them have excellent conversation skills but pretty limited nonverbal skills. Using both of these communication skills is necessary for building healthy, deep, and long-lasting intimate friendships, relationships, and a strong social support network. This is what we mental health professionals call "self-care." But there's another aspect to healthy communication people are often surprised by: assertiveness.

People unfamiliar with assertiveness have three words in common—"sure," "yes," and "fine." Nice men and women use these words to cushion themselves from conflict. But nice comes with a price. You may be described as generous, accessible, and extremely polite, but are likely to be plagued with anxiety, loneliness, and loads of resentments. Becoming assertive is not simply a practice, it's a downright art.

Remember those beliefs we covered? In my experience, becoming more assertive requires some serious, and sometimes messy, belief-challenging.

Being Assertive

Being more assertive takes time, effort, and commitment. Be kind to yourself and start small. Tally up some quick wins by practicing one or two small gestures of assertiveness. You could do this by saying no to an outing you don't want to go on, choosing what you order for dinner instead of saying "anything is fine," or choosing not to apologize for something that isn't your fault. Like anything else, assertiveness will take practice.

CREATING BOUNDARIES

Our personal boundaries are the mental picket fences marking where we stop and another person begins. They come from our core values, and more importantly, the values we place on ourselves and our well-being. Poor or lacking personal boundaries can be tracked to how we received love and attention from our parents and caregivers, and are greatly influenced by how we learned to get our basic needs met.

Boundaries are what make us emotionally and psychically safe; it is the space between us and another. They protect our mental well-being and allow for a healthy expression of who we are. Each boundary we set builds our self-confidence and esteem more profoundly than any other interpersonal interaction. The most generous, effective, and loving people in our world have the strongest boundaries. They allow others to feel safe because they know where others stand. They show others how much they value themselves because they are willing to protect their self-worth.

With boundaries, we allow ourselves to give what we want or can, instead of giving too much and burning out.

Now, in Week Five, the culmination of your practice becomes centered on the benefits of communicating your boundaries in a healthy way.

SETTING BOUNDARIES IN TWO STEPS

This is where your assertive communication skills become important. Life is messy and boundaries are one of the messiest parts of life.

STEP ONE

Good, solid communication relies heavily on listening skills. First, listen hard to yourself. Explore your needs and align them with your values. Then listen to your intuition. This might be the most important part of setting your boundaries.

You can save yourself a lot of trouble, anger, and headaches if you know when to say "no" before boundary crossing becomes an issue. Remember this moment, because it will save you a lot of heartache moving forward. *You have every right in the world to say no.* Be diligent about who you allow in your space. For example:

If you value punctuality, then being on a team with someone who is habitually late is setting yourself up for crossed boundaries.

If you value financial well-being, then dating a big spender is setting yourself up for crossed boundaries.

If you know that you value cooperation, then being best friends with someone who is selfish is setting yourself up for crossed boundaries.

Knowing what you will and won't tolerate allows you to avoid getting into situations where boundaries might be crossed from the start. This is not to say that you shouldn't engage with people who don't share the same values as you. It is just to say, make sure you know the playing field that you are stepping into.

Oftentimes, someone will have values we don't agree with, but they will have other qualities that redeem them so we can't help but love them. We accept them and move ahead, doing our best to make it work.

STEP TWO

This is the part where you teach people how to treat you. Remember, this is messy stuff. Along the way you are inevitably going to get your toes stepped on, but you can drastically reduce the number of times and the frequency with which this happens by getting good at communicating your boundaries.

The key to successfully setting boundaries is having clear expectations and learning the power of your own voice. An unverbalized boundary is not a boundary. People don't know they've crossed a boundary if you don't tell them you have one. No matter how much we think others should know what we are thinking, they simply can't always know where the line is.

Using this technique, you will allow yourself to thoughtfully develop, prepare, and practice setting a full and complete set of boundaries. I highly recommend you write this out and carry it with you.

Expand Your "I" Statement

Strong "I" statements have five specific elements:

1. Feeling

2. Behavior

3. Tangible effect (consequence to you)

4. Need

5. Tangible effect (consequence to them)

*It does not need to be a nuclear bomb type of consequence.

Example: "I feel frustrated when you are late for meetings. I don't like having to repeat information, so I need you to be on time. If you cannot be on time, please let me know before the meeting, or I will cancel our meeting and move onto another task."

That is really it. Read, rinse, and repeat, as the saying goes.

COMMUNICATION AND RELATIONSHIP PATTERNS

Relationship patterns come in many flavors, some good and some not so good. How about the push and pull of a cycle of breakups and makeups? These scripted and mostly toxic roles draw us into difficult-to-break and comfortable-to-repeat patterns rooted in our early development and attachments. These patterns offer comfort in a predictable style of relating and communicating that slowly chips away at our emotional safety and self-esteem.

In order to interrupt these patterns, we need to review the skill of cultivating awareness of our feelings and putting together a plan for better communication.

If you want to stop some of your unhealthy relationship patterns, then you need to practice—you guessed it!—healthy communication. A good rule of thumb for any relationship that encounters problems is for you to take a beat before you respond. That could mean an extra moment to breathe and gather your thoughts or taking a day of space to assess how you feel. Think of which feeling you'd like to convey. Here's the catch: It can't be the feeling "angry." If you're in a disagreement, you almost certainly feel angry, but what is it masking? Fear? Sadness? Take some time to identify that feeling, then choose an "I" statement to express yourself.

Many life events cause stress in our relationships well beyond the daily rituals of living. One of the most challenging aspects is a topic I have threaded throughout this book: When the people closest to us respond to uncomfortable situations and feelings with fear, discomfort, and distraction, they move away from intimacy. And as we move away from connection, we lose sight of our needs and our ability to sustain a future built on healthy self-esteem and confidence.

CELEBRATE SUCCESS

Congratulations! You have made it through all five weeks of the program! Hopefully you have learned more about your relationship with yourself, how to set achievable and realistic goals, and the techniques and tools for meeting and confronting your inner critic. These tools can transform your relationship with your thoughts, helping you understand your abilities and behaviors and how they are influenced by your values and beliefs, and be used as powerful and effective ways of communicating your needs and wants. I know you have worked hard to uncover and tackle some distinctly uncomfortable stuff to move toward your goals for better self-confidence and self-esteem.

Not quite feeling it yet? Yeah, that can happen. No need for discouragement or surrendering to a full-on invasion of your inner critic. You are here, still reading and showing up, which means that you are still curious about improving yourself. Oh, how I wish building self-esteem and confidence were as easy as turning on a light. It's more like lighting a whole room of candles—it seems unattainable and slow, but so very beautiful and magical when you finish.

You may not yet be where you would like to see yourself, but I am not going to stop now. Are you with me? Let's take a moment to ask a few questions to check for self-improvement.

Have you felt that your confidence and esteem has improved since beginning this book?

Has anyone complimented you?

Have you experienced any rewards, such as calmer days or better sleep?

Is your mood lighter?

How often have you smiled in the last week?

How many good days have you had in the last five weeks?

Just in case you need a bit more motivation, I have created a bonus week to assist you in progressing even further on your path to your more confident and esteem-filled future. I'll walk you through proven ways for continuing to build and practice what you have learned, how to refocus your goals when needed, and simple tips for when you need a boost to keep moving forward. Onward we go!

CHAPTER 8
After Week Five – Your Confident Future

Well, here we are! I want you to know that it doesn't matter if you have gotten here in five weeks or five months. You are here, and that is what counts! My hope is that you have found this book to be a helpful pathway toward better self-confidence and self-esteem *for you*. I encourage you to look back on what you have learned and establish some kind of daily practice using the work you have done within each of the weekly sessions as your outline for moving forward. It is very much okay if you did not complete every exercise or identify with all of the information. Learning is not linear; you decide your own start and finish lines. You should encourage yourself to meander to and fro and retrace your steps if you need to.

Personal growth and development of self-confidence and self-esteem cannot be confined by a simplistic idea of a start and finish line. Why on earth would we want it to be that way? Let's explore the meandering path most of us take, and the places we encounter blocks and how to climb over them.

THE SIX REASONS WE GET STUCK

TIME

Sure, Rome wasn't built in a day, but that was in 753 BCE! Today, your video/quote/blog can go viral overnight and suddenly you are "relevant." This type of "success" may give you a boost in self-confidence, but will definitely challenge you in other ways, especially if you have not done some of the work in this book. Most of us initiate change due to some sort of setback, be it personal or professional. We expect our progress to be a straight upward line of improvement, making us feel better and better each day. These unrealistic and often excessive expectations are a primary cause of low self-confidence and esteem. The solution comes from setting *achievable goals.*

SELF-JUDGMENT

We move toward change from internal desire, and our inner critic says, "Oh no you don't, it doesn't feel right yet!" My Negative Nelly still tries to tell me that I can only do things if I am in a "positive" mood or state of mind. She likes to put me in a holding pattern of feeling good about whatever I want to change. She keeps me stuck on purpose and makes me equate motivation with an acceptable "good" emotion. Well, if you're like me, change is mostly scary and uncomfortable, not always exciting and fun! I know if Nelly is loud and proud, I need to get committed to doing the opposite of what she tells me. The solution to harsh self-judgment is *self-acceptance and self-encouragement.*

FEAR

Fear is a normal feeling when one of our internalized threats is triggered. It is an automated response—unless we become aware of it and change the momentum. We numb ourselves to it, hoping it will just go away. But the truth is that it won't, and we often end up remaining comfortable in our discomfort. Coping with our fears in this way takes us further from ourselves, creating fertile ground for distorted thinking. By allowing fear to go unexamined, without learning the feeling below the fear, it will fester, leading to negative effects on our minds, bodies, and spirits. The solution to fear is *learning to challenge our thoughts and better define our feelings.*

SKILLS

To be skillful at something requires some practice. What we practice is what we get good at. Do you hide behind often self-constructed labels like type-A, perfectionist, or super mom/dad? How do you practice these labels? The more curious you get about your relationship with yourself, the more you will step back and challenge these labels. This curiosity will help you develop your daily practice of whatever skills you choose to prioritize, from your history or from this book. If reading a good self-help book alone got anyone to their goal, I would probably not be writing this one, because everyone would've been cured years ago. Skill-building in any area of life requires practice. Twenty years and three guitars later, I still cannot play more than five chords, because I don't prioritize practicing the guitar. But I have gained many other skills by going back to school, becoming a counselor, finding recovery, and improving my self-esteem. An obvious solution to lack of skills is *learning and practicing some new ones.*

DIFFICULT CHOICES

What do I believe? What do I value? How do I want to behave and live? The principles you live by are your choice. Understanding how and why we developed our beliefs and values allows us to choose whether to keep living with them or not. We get to look below the surface of our habits and discover our true self. If we are making life decisions based only on the values and beliefs that were passed down to us, if we automatically accept them as good and correct, have we really made a decision? Can you go on feeling as though your insides do not match your outsides? I could not, so I made a choice to learn what I truly believed and valued. The solution to difficult choices is *making one and understanding why you did.*

QUITTING

Resting, reassuring, relying, refocusing, referring, reflecting, and reassessing are not quitting words, they are growing words. Life is hard work, and changing something deep within us, such as our confidence and self-worth, is not easy. I encourage you to pay attention to when you need time to practice the seven Rs:

Rest your mind.
Reassure yourself that you are doing the right thing.
Rely on someone else for a moment.
Refocus on your strengths.
Refer back to this book.
Reflect on what has been working for you and what has not.
Reassessing is the solution to quitting.

REFLECTING ON YOUR GOALS

Do you remember the list of incredible things that are possible from the Beginning Your Journey chapter?

* You will enjoy, like, and value yourself.
* You will be able to make better decisions.
* You will take the time you need to learn to be with yourself.
* You will handle mistakes without blaming yourself or others unfairly.
* You will be able to assert yourself without feeling guilty.
* You will recognize, name, and accept your strengths and weaknesses.
* You will show kindness and compassion toward yourself.
* You will believe you are good enough and that you matter.
* You will discover what you want and need, and learn to believe that you deserve these things in life.

I invite you to look back at what goals you developed from this list in Week One. What did you hope to gain by reading this book? How did you move through the book? What resonated and what didn't? What feelings arose and when? These are the questions of self-assessment, and there are no "right" answers. Take a moment to breathe and discern if you feel any different or are thinking differently. Has anything shifted inside of you? Has anyone noticed something new in your actions? By asking these questions, you can rework and redefine your goals for the future.

YOUR SUSTAINABLE SELF-ESTEEM: THE ACT AND FEAR ACRONYMS

While I've included both CBT and ACT throughout the book, ACT gives us specific tools that are extraordinarily useful in moving toward long-term, sustainable self-improvement. The techniques that follow are geared toward the A and C of ACT (which, you'll recall, stands for Acceptance and Commitment Therapy). It means noticing and accepting thoughts, events, and interactions, especially the uncomfortable ones—such as when we don't change as quickly or easily as we or others want—then committing to clarifying our personal values and taking action. We do this to increase our flexibility and ability to cope with circumstances in more authentic and creative ways. To be clear, this is not multitasking with our minds, switching between tasks and thoughts. Psychological flexibility is about learning how to adapt in healthier ways to the demands of day-to-day life and commit to practicing new ways of behaving.

ACT is based on the core concept that we humans are pretty rigid in our psychological processes, triggering internal incongruency and failure to behave in alignment with our core values. Practicing the steps below is one tool for coping with our rigid natures.

ACT
* Accept your reactions and be present.
* Choose a valued direction.
* Take action.

Steps to using ACT:

1. Acceptance is an alternative to our instinct to avoid thinking about negative—or potentially negative—experiences. Start by taking in a deep breath, observing your present state of mind, and letting thoughts come and go using positive self-talk, such as, "They are just thoughts, not facts. They will pass." Acknowledge what you can control and ride the wave of feelings over what you cannot.

2. Consider your values—which one works for this situation? Choose and commit to a direction/solution based on your values.

3. Keep your values in mind as you take action. Continue to make choices by doing the things that support you and your values.

As you continue to develop a deeper understanding of what your values are and what specific goals you have set to live those values, it is important to become aware of the barriers that will inevitably arise. Then, you can build and practice coping skills to deal with them.

ACT uses the acronym F-E-A-R (fusion, evaluation, avoidance, and reason-giving) to help us better understand these barriers. I have outlined my own definitions for these core barriers below.

* Fusion (of unhelpful thoughts with unexpressed feelings)
* Evaluation (high expectations with limited resources or time, skills, and assistance)
* Avoidance (numbing or distracting yourself from feeling uncomfortable)
* Reason-giving (blaming unexamined beliefs and values)

Steps to using FEAR:

1. Reduce the habit of believing your thoughts to be facts. Notice them without becoming entangled in them.

2. Summarize why your thoughts are not realistic and are potentially problematic.

3. Investigate what you avoid in life and the consequences of doing so, such as numbing yourself with alcohol, drugs, or other behaviors.

4. Examine how giving reasons may be harmful. Ask yourself why you can't, won't, or shouldn't change, and why your life cannot be improved.

YOUR IMPROVED WELL-BEING: PERSEVERANCE AND SELF-COMPASSION

The research is clear: There is a strong and important connection between applied self-compassion and increased perseverance toward self-improvement. Dr. Kristin Neff, a leader in the research and application of compassion-based therapy, defines self-compassion as an attitude that involves treating oneself with warmth and understanding in difficult times, and recognizing that making mistakes is a part of being human. Self-compassion supports our self-esteem but differs in one very important area: You can be compassionate with yourself even if you don't really feel all that great about yourself or what you have done. The act of being compassionate with yourself improves your internal motivation to continue on your self-improvement journey!

Tips for practicing self-compassion:

Allow yourself to make mistakes. Show yourself kindness and understanding when you do human things like break a dish, trip over nothing, or miss an appointment. If you call yourself a name, immediately and purposefully correct yourself with a kinder statement, such as, "You are allowed to be human, Lynn," or "I still love you, girl!" Show yourself love.

Treat yourself as you treat your best friend. Pat yourself, hold your own hand, or even give yourself a big hug! Use the language of kindness, tenderness, and forgiveness with yourself. Terms of sweetness and endearment—like "sweetie," "sweet thang," or "baby cakes"—are my personal favorites.

Tell yourself good things as a release from your critical self-talk. Try out, "It is okay that I feel angry and upset right now."

Motivate yourself without "shoulding" all over everything. Ask yourself what you are criticizing yourself for, and open your heart and mind to the feelings beneath the expectation of what should be happening. Think about how you would nurture a child, and try to reframe your inner dialogue to be less judgmental toward yourself.

SIMPLE WAYS TO REFOCUS OR GET A QUICK BOOST

We all need a little something sometimes in order to keep going on any journey of change. These exercises and techniques can help you regain perspective and activate your motivation to keep moving forward in building your self-confidence and self-esteem.

DEFINE WHAT INTEGRITY MEANS FOR YOU

Sometimes when you feel guilty and drained it is due to living life without personal honesty, sincerity, and trustworthiness. What are your ethical and moral codes? Are you living them today?

LISTEN TO SOME BOSS BASS

When you want to feel empowered, listen to empowering music. A study led by Adam Galinsky and Dennis Y. Hsu from the Kellogg School of Management at Northwestern University shows that bass-heavy music can make you feel more confident.

These were the most powerful songs from the study:

1. "We Will Rock You" by Queen

2. "Get Ready for This" by 2 Unlimited

3. "In Da Club" by 50 Cent

GET YOUR LUCK ON

Sure enough, researchers have shown that lucky charms actually do the job! Well, it was more around activating superstition, but either way, it works. Grab your rabbit foot keychain or special something and get lucky!

PICK A QUOTE AND TURN IT INTO YOUR MANTRA

✳ "Life is ten percent what you experience and ninety percent how you respond to it." –Dorothy M. Neddermeyer

✳ "Think like a queen. A queen is not afraid to fail. Failure is another stepping stone to greatness." –Oprah Winfrey

✳ "You are the only person on earth who can use your ability." –Zig Ziglar

✳ "Self-confidence is the memory of success." –David Storey

✳ "No one can make you feel inferior without your consent." –Eleanor Roosevelt

If you don't connect with any of these quotes, go ahead and find one, or even make one up that works for you!

SETTING BIGGER GOALS

As you continue to learn and grow through the many aspects of self-confidence and self-esteem, you may begin to think of yourself as fully changed or even healed. Many of us buy into this idea and may then move on to the next part of ourselves that needs to be "fixed." Such is the never-ending damaging cycle of viewing ourselves as broken. The goal of being "better" is actually a form of distorted thinking, polarizing us to believe we need to be all or nothing. Yikes, who wants that?!

What if instead you extend your goal from being, "fixed, done, or healed" to "I am healing, growing, and learning"? What would happen if you took these five weeks of learning, practicing, and improving, and then kept on going? Learning is, after all, a lifelong event. And it rewards us not only with knowledge but also with improved esteem and confidence. You know, a win-win situation!

SUSTAINING YOUR SELF-CONFIDENCE AND ESTEEM

Life is going to keep happening on its own terms. We are not going to be suddenly or forever immune to fears, self-doubt, and the uncontrollable things in our world. It is during the difficult times that we are better able to prioritize our personal growth. With every "two steps forward, one step back" situation, we can learn to accept and embrace the nonlinear reality of authentic and sustainable forward momentum. I want to leave you with a final list for those with either ambivalence or ambition. The most relevant aspect of any journey is progress, not perfection.

Find your path: Become clearer and more curious in determining your personal path. Each of us must find and practice our unique way forward. If someone tries to sell you a "one size fits all" approach, please don't buy it.

Focus: What you focus on will become your reality. If you focus on predicting and preparing for the worst, your energy and time will flow in the direction of catastrophe.

Be with yourself: Give consistent time and attention toward yourself and your needs and you *will* see and feel results. Having a well-established foundational practice keeps us grounded in our strengths when life sends us lemons and curveballs.

Adjust your expectations: Your personal investment may not provide an "equal or greater" return. Look at the results as worthy as opposed to "not enough."

Trust and love the process: This is a courageous road not traveled by anyone but you. It is a path paved with small stones of self-love and possibilities. The less you fixate on the destination, the more you will be content and joyful along the way.

RESOURCES

ONLINE RESOURCES

Visit the following online resources to enhance your learning, to find professional help, and to dive deeper into treatments and techniques.

GENERAL INFORMATION ANXIETY AND DEPRESSION ASSOCIATION OF AMERICA (ADAA)

http://www.adaa.org/understanding-anxiety

The ADAA website discusses what distinguishes normal anxiety and depression from a disorder, provides statistics about these conditions, and has information about OCD and PTSD.

MAYO CLINIC HEALTHY LIFESTYLE

www.mayoclinic.org/healthy-lifestyle

The Mayo Clinic offers overviews on healthy eating, fitness, stress management, weight loss, and other topics. More in-depth articles are available under each subject heading.

NATIONAL INSTITUTE OF MENTAL HEALTH (NIMH)

Anxiety: www.nimh.nih.gov/health/topics/anxiety-disorders/index.shtml

Depression: www.nimh.nih.gov/health/topics/depression/index.shtml

These websites describe common symptoms of depression and anxiety, and discuss risk factors, treatments, and how to find clinical trials you might qualify for. They also include links to free booklets and brochures.

NATIONAL INSTITUTE ON ALCOHOL ABUSE AND ALCOHOLISM (NIAAA)

www.niaaa.nih.gov

The NIAAA website provides information about the effects of consuming alcohol, describes ongoing research trials, and includes information about clinical trials you might be eligible for. It also includes links to free pamphlets, brochures, and fact sheets.

ANXIETY AND DEPRESSION ASSOCIATION OF AMERICA (ADAA)

www.adaa.org/supportgroups

The ADAA provides information about support groups by state (as well as some international listings), including contact information for these groups.

FIND A CBT THERAPIST—ASSOCIATION FOR BEHAVIORAL AND COGNITIVE THERAPIES (ABCT)

www.findcbt.org

This website of the leading professional organization for CBT therapists and researchers allows you to search for CBT therapists by ZIP code, specialty, and accepted insurance.

NATIONAL ALLIANCE ON MENTAL ILLNESS (NAMI)

www.nami.org/Find-Support

The NAMI website offers ways to find support for you or a loved one who has a psychological disorder. Many additional resources are available on the site, including links to local NAMI chapters.

NATIONAL SUICIDE PREVENTION LIFELINE

www.suicidepreventionlifeline.org or call 1-800-273-8255

The lifeline provides free and confidential support 24 hours a day, every day of the year. Phone and online chat options are available.

PSYCHOLOGICAL TREATMENTS—ASSOCIATION FOR BEHAVIORAL AND COGNITIVE THERAPIES (ABCT)

www.abct.org/Information/?m=mInformation&fa=_psychoTreatments

This website covers topics such as evidence-based practice, treatment options, and choosing a therapist.

RESEARCH-SUPPORTED TREATMENTS—SOCIETY OF CLINICAL PSYCHOLOGY (SCP)

www.div12.org/psychological-treatments/

Division 12 of the American Psychological Association, the SCP, keeps a list of research-supported psychological treatments. The website is searchable by treatment and psychological condition.

SUBSTANCE ABUSE AND MENTAL HEALTH SERVICES ADMINISTRATION (SAMHSA)

www.findtreatment.samhsa.gov/

The SAMHSA is part of the US Department of Health and Human Services and offers many resources for those who are struggling with addiction, including a treatment services locator.

MINDFULNESS AMERICAN MINDFULNESS RESEARCH ASSOCIATION (AMRA)

www.goamra.org

The AMRA presents the latest mindfulness-related research findings, as well as an interactive map for finding mindfulness training programs.

MINDFULNET

www.mindfulnet.org/

This website is a clearinghouse of information about mindfulness: what it is, how it's used, research that supports it, and more. Many of their books are on the Association for Behavioral and Cognitive Therapy's Books of Merit list, meaning they present a treatment that is based on solid research evidence. The full list can be found at www.abct.org/SHBooks.

LITERATURE

ADDICTION

Anderson, Kenneth. *How to Change Your Drinking: A Harm Reduction Guide to Alcohol.* New York: The HAMS Harm Reduction Network, 2010.

Glasner-Edwards, Suzette, PhD. *The Addiction Recovery Skills Workbook: Changing Addictive Behaviors Using CBT, Mindfulness, and Motivational Interviewing Techniques.* Oakland: New Harbinger Publications, 2015.

Williams, Rebecca, and Julie Kraft. *The Mindfulness Workbook for Addiction: A Guide to Coping with the Grief, Stress, and Anger that Trigger Addictive Behaviors.* Oakland: New Harbinger Publications, 2012.

Wilson, Kelley, and Troy DuFrene. *The Wisdom to Know the Difference: An Acceptance and Commitment Therapy Workbook for Overcoming Substance Abuse.* Oakland: New Harbinger Publications, 2012.

ANGER

Karmin, Aaron. *Anger Management Workbook for Men: Take Control of Your Anger and Master Your Emotions.* Berkeley: Althea Press, 2016.

McKay, Matthew, and Peter Rogers. *The Anger Control Workbook.* Oakland: New Harbinger Publications, 2000.

Potter-Efron, Ronald. *Rage: A Step-by-Step Guide to Overcoming Explosive Anger.* Oakland: New Harbinger Publications, 2007.

ANXIETY

Antony, Martin M., and Richard P. Swinson. *The Shyness and Social Anxiety Workbook: Proven Techniques for Overcoming Your Fears.* Oakland: New Harbinger Publications, 2017.

Carbonell, David. *Panic Attacks Workbook: A Guided Program for Beating the Panic Trick.* Berkeley: Ulysses Press, 2004.

Clark, David A., and Aaron T. Beck. *The Anxiety and Worry Workbook: The Cognitive Behavioral Solution.* New York: The Guilford Press, 2011.

Cuncic, Arlin. *The Anxiety Workbook: A 7-Week Plan to Overcome Anxiety, Stop Worrying, and End Panic.* Berkeley: Althea Press, 2017.

Robichaud, Melisa, and Michel J. Dugas. *The Generalized Anxiety Disorder Workbook: A Comprehensive CBT Guide for Coping with Uncertainty, Worry, and Fear.* Oakland: New Harbinger Publications, 2015.

Tolin, David. *Face Your Fears: A Proven Plan to Beat Anxiety, Panic, Phobias, and Obsessions.* Hoboken, NJ: Wiley, 2012.

Tompkins, Michael A. *Anxiety and Avoidance: A Universal Treatment for Anxiety, Panic, and Fear.* Oakland: New Harbinger Publications, 2017.

ASSERTIVENESS

Alberti, Robert, and Michael Emmons. *Your Perfect Right: Assertiveness and Equality in Your Life and Relationships.* Atascadero, CA: Impact, 2107.

Vavrichek, Sherrie. *The Guide to Compassionate Assertiveness: How to Express Your Needs and Deal with Conflict while Keeping a Kind Heart.* Oakland: New Harbinger Publications, 2012.

DEPRESSION

Davis, Martha, Elizabeth Robbins Eshelman, and Matthew McKay. *The Relaxation and Stress Reduction Workbook,* 6th ed. Oakland: New Harbinger Publications, 2019.

Ellis, Albert, and Robert A. Harper. *A New Guide to Rational Living.* Wilshire Book Company, 1975.

Gillihan, Seth J. *Retrain Your Brain: Cognitive Behavioral Therapy in 7 Weeks: A Workbook for Managing Depression and Anxiety.* Althea Press, 2016.

Otto, Michael and Jasper Smits. *Exercise for Mood and Anxiety: Proven Strategies for Overcoming Depression and Enhancing Well-Being.* Oxford University Press, 2009.

MINDFULNESS

Brach, Tara. *Radical Acceptance: Embracing Your Life with the Heart of a Buddha.* Tantor Audio, January 17, 2012.

Germer, Christopher K. *The Mindful Path to Self-Compassion: Freeing Yourself from Destructive Thoughts and Emotions.* Tantor Audio, 2016.

Kabat-Zinn, Jon. *Full Catastrophe Living: Using the Wisdom of Your Body and Mind to Face Stress, Pain, and Illness, Revised ed.* Random House, 2007.

Orsillo, Susan M., and Lizabeth Roemer. *The Mindful Way through Anxiety: Break Free from Chronic Worry and Reclaim Your Life.* The New York: Guilford Press, 2011.

Salzberg, Sharon. *Lovingkindness: The Revolutionary Art of Happiness.* Boston: Shambhala, 2002.

RELATIONSHIPS

Gottman, John, and Joan DeClaire. *The Relationship Cure: A Five-Step Guide to Strengthening Your Marriage, Family, and Friendships.* New York: Harmony, 2002.

McKay, Matthew, Patrick Fanning, and Kim Paleg. *Couple Skills: Making Your Relationship Work.* Oakland: New Harbinger Publications, 2006.

Ruiz, Don Miguel. *The Mastery of Love: A Practical Guide to the Art of Relationship.* San Rafael, CA: Amber-Allen Publishing, 1999.

SELF-CARE

Brown, Brené. *The Gifts of Imperfection: Let Go of Who You Think You're Supposed to Be and Embrace Who You Are.* Center City, MN: Hazelden Publishing, 2010.

Neff, Kristin. *Self-Compassion: The Proven Power of Being Kind to Yourself.* New York: William Morrow, 2016.

SLEEP

Carney, Colleen. *Quiet Your Mind and Get to Sleep: Solutions to Insomnia for Those with Depression, Anxiety, or Chronic Pain.* Oakland: New Harbinger Publications, 2009.

Ehrnstrom, Colleen, and Alisha L. Brosse. *End the Insomnia Struggle: A Step-by-Step Guide to Help You Get to Sleep and Stay Asleep.* Oakland: New Harbinger Publications, 2016.

REFERENCES

Baumeister, Roy F., Jennifer D. Campbell, Joachim I. Krueger, and Kathleen D. Vohs. "Does High Self-Esteem Cause Better Performance, Interpersonal Success, Happiness, or Healthier Lifestyles?" *Psychological Science in the Public Interest* 4, no. 1 (May 2003): 1–44.

Beck, Aaron. *Cognitive Therapies and Emotional Disorders*. New York: New American Library, 1976.

Beck, Aaron. "Good Therapy." Good Therapy LLC. Last modified July 8, 2015. www.goodtherapy.org/famous-psychologists/aaron-beck.html.

Beck, Judith S. *Cognitive Behavioral Therapy*. New York: Guilford Press, 2011.

Bratman, Gregory N., et al. "Nature Experience Reduces Rumination and Subgenual Prefrontal Cortex Activation." *PNAS* 112, no. 28 (2015): 8567–8572. doi:10.1073/pnas.1510459112.

Burns, Cynthia. "Expectancy and Self-focused Attention: Experimental Support for the Self-Regulation Model of Test Anxiety." *Journal of Social and Clinical Psychology* 7: (2006) 246–59.

Burns, David D. *Feeling Good: The New Mood Therapy*. New York: New American Library, 1980.

Burns, David D. *The Feeling Good Handbook*. New York: Morrow, 1989.

Burns, David D., Brian F. Shaw and William Croker. "Thinking Styles and Coping Strategies of Depressed Women: An Empirical Investigation." *Behaviour Research and Therapy* 25 (1987): 223-225. doi:10.1016/0005-7967(87)90049-0.

Earley, Jay, and Weiss, Bonnie. *Self-Therapy for Your Inner Critic: Transforming Self-Criticism into Self-Confidence.* Larkspur, CA: Pattern System Books, 2010.

Harris, Russ. *The Happiness Trap: How to Stop Struggling and Start Living.* Boston: Trumpeter Books, 2008.

Hayes, Steven C., Kirk D. Strosahl, and Kelly G. Wilson. *Acceptance and Commitment Therapy: An Experiential Approach to Behavior Change.* New York: Guilford Press, 1999.

Hsu, Dennis Y., Li Huang, Loran Nordgren, Derek Rucker, and Adam D. Galinsky. "The Music of Power: Perceptual and Behavioral Consequences of Powerful Music." *Social Psychological and Personality Science* (2015) 6(1), 75–83.

Jones, G., A. B. J. Swain, and L. Hardy. "Intensity and Direction Dimensions of Competitive State Anxiety and Relationships with Performance." *Journal of Sport Sciences* (1993) 11: 525–32.

Jones, G., S. Hanton, and A. B. J. Swain. "Intensity and Interpretation of Anxiety Symptoms in Elite and Non-elite Sports Performers." *Personality and Individual Differences* 17: (1994) 657–63.

Krieger, Seth. "Positive Self-Statements: Power for Some, Peril for Others." *Psychological Science* 20, no. 7 (July 2012): 860–66.

Latham, Gary P. and T. W. Lee. *Goal Setting: In Generalizing from Laboratory to Field Settings: Research Findings for Industrial-Organizational Psychology, Organizational Behavior, and Human Resource Management.* Lexington, MA: Lexington Books, 1986.

Malone Johanna, Sabrina R. Liu, George E. Vaillant, Dorene M. Rentz, and Robert J. Waldinger. "Midlife Eriksonian Psychosocial Development: Setting the Stage for Late-Life Cognitive and Emotional Health." *Developmental Psychology* 52, no. 3 (2016): 496–508. doi:10.1037/a0039875.

Massey, Morris. "Values Development." *Changing Minds. Wikipedia, The Free Encyclopedia.* Accessed January 3, 2011.

Morin, Amy. *Things Mentally Strong People Don't Do.* London: Harper, 2013.

Morsella, Ezequiel, Christine A. Godwin, Tiffany K. Jantz, and Stephen C. Krieger. "Homing in on Consciousness in the Nervous System: An Action-Based Synthesis." *Behavioral and Brain Sciences 39*, no. e168. (2016) doi:10.1017/S0140525X15000643.

National Institute of Mental Health. "Any Mental Illness (AMI) Among Adults." Accessed May 1, 2019. www.nimh.nih.gov/health/statistics/mental-illness.shtml#part_154785.

Neff, Kristin D. "Development and Validation of a Scale to Measure Self-Compassion." *Self and Identity,* 2 (2003): 223–250.

Neff, Kristin. "Self-Compassion: An Alternative Conceptualization of a Healthy Attitude toward Oneself." *Self and Identity* 2, no. 2 (2003): 85–101.

Norwood, G. *Maslow's Hierarchy of Needs: A Theory of Human Motivation.* Martino Fine Books, 2009.

Oettingen, Gabriele, Gaby Hönig, and Peter M. Gollwitzer. "Effective Self-Regulation of Goal Attainment." *International Journal of Educational Research 33*, no. 7–8 (2015): 705–732.

Prochaska, James O., John Norcross, and Carlo DiClemente. *Changing for Good: A Revolutionary Six-Stage Program for Overcoming Bad Habits and Moving Your Life Positively Forward.* New York: Willliam Morrow, 1994.

Pyszczynski, Tom, and Jeff Greenberg. *Hanging On and Letting Go: Understanding the Onset, Progression, and Remission of Depression.* New York: Springer Science & Business Media, 2012.

Sage, Nigel, Michelle Sowden, Elizabeth Chorlton, and Andrea Edeleanu. *CBT for Chronic Illness and Palliative Care: A Workbook and Toolkit*. John Wiley & Sons, 2013.

Vogel-Scibilia Suzanne, Kathryn McNulty, Beth Baxter, Steve Miller, Max Dine, and Frederick Frese. "The Recovery Process Utilizing Erikson's Stages of Human Development." *Community Mental Health*, January 12, 2009.

INDEX

ACKNOWLEDGMENTS

In July of 2010, I found my way back to me. After 20 years of numbing my true self with alcohol and anti-anxiety medication, I found abstinence, sobriety, and recovery. I would like to thank the many friends and family members who helped me through that terrifying and uncomfortable process, and who today, near and far, continue to love me and cheer me on to be better at just being me. Without these people, I would not have been able to rebuild my life from the inside out, much less write this book.

ABOUT THE AUTHOR

Lynn Matti, MA, LPCC, is a Person-Centered and Cognitive Behavioral Licensed Professional Clinical Counselor, Addiction/Sobriety/Recovery Coach, advocate, and leader who teaches online and in-person at the intersection of resilience, courage, and hope. She's known for the quirkiness, wisdom, and authenticity she brings professionally and personally, and the tested, interesting, and fun practices and perspectives she brings to her individual clients and group endeavors.

In addition to a thriving Peachtree City, GA private practice, Lynn is the host of *The SoberSoul Recovery Podcast* and creator of SoberSoul Recovery, an online all-inclusive lifestyle and learning and connecting environment for men and women who desire true transformation. In this space, she mentors and supports people recovering from low self-esteem/confidence, grief, anxiety, depression, relocation, divorce, loneliness, substance overuse, and substance use disorders.

She has been featured most recently on Bustle.com, *Recovery Today Magazine*, and Recovery.org.

Learn more about Lynn on her websites: LynnMatti.com and SoberSoulRecovery.net.